Miss Taylor Meets Mr. Burton

"The way I began falling in love with Richard was very funny, really. He was kind of a legend in the theater and in films. . . .

"I had met Richard before at Stewart Granger's house. My first impression was that he was rather full of himself. I seemed to remember that he never stopped talking and I had given him the cold fish eye. So I figured that now Richard would come along, the Old Vic actor, and sort of throw the cues to Rex if he dried up and before I even opened my mouth he'd probably be throwing me my cues. . . .

"Well, the first day we were to work together I've never seen a gentleman so hung over in my whole life. . . .

"Then when it was time to do some work, he blew a line. If it had been a planned strategic campaign, Caesar couldn't have planned it better. My heart just went out to him."

ELIZABETH TAYLOR
An Informal Memoir
by
Elizabeth Taylor
with
Photographs by Roddy McDowall
plus a
Collection from Elizabeth Taylor's
Family Album

AN AVON BOOK

AVON BOOKS
A division of
The Hearst Corporation
959 Eighth Avenue
New York, N. Y. 10019

First Avon Printing, January, 1967

Cover photo by Bert Stern

Pricted in the U.S.A.

To the lady from Pismo Beach

I want to thank Richard Burton for marrying me; and Richard Meryman for his help and his tape recorder.

I MUST CONFESS I have very mixed feelings about this book. There's always a terrible danger when you talk about yourself of sounding like you're trying to capitalize on your emotions, your relationships. Or it may sound as if I'm trying to justify myself. I have made horrendous mistakes in my life, but I cannot blame them on anybody else. We all have to participate in our own downfalls. Excuses cannot absolve you, and they are so undignified. Let's face it—my life seems to have lacked dignity. Maybe I shouldn't add to it by going into things that don't belong to the public.

And there is a point of privacy beyond which I simply will not go, because it would involve throwing mud. My reluctance isn't a matter of ethics, really.

It's realism. The person who throws the mud is always reduced.

On the other hand, perhaps I have been in the public eye too long. I am disgusted by the amount of myth that now is accepted as fact. The public me, the one named Elizabeth Taylor, has become a lot of hokum and fabrication—a bunch of drivel—and I find her slightly revolting.

This book is probably best described not as an autobiography—that's much too pretentious—but as a long, slightly overcozy conversation with a garrulous broad named Betty Burton. I have no doubt that a lot of it will seem rather like a bad novelette. I'm afraid much of my life has been a cliche—except that at the time the feelings were tremendously deep.

In my life, I have never, God knows, done anything by half-measures. I have never thought we should avoid what life dishes out to us. I believe people are like rocks formed by the weather. We're formed by experience, by heartache, by grief, by mistakes, by guilt, by shame—all the things that psychiatrists would like to take off our shoulders. But how do you become a full-fledged human being without taking the brunt head on? I am glad that in my life I have never cut short my emotions. The most awful thing of all is to be numb.

My earliest memory is of pain. In the house in London where I was born, there was one of those electric fires that coils and curls. I was still crawling and I remember looking at its marvelous orangey-red color and thinking, Should I or shouldn't I? I did. Thank you very much! Half a finger almost burned off!

I remember too—I must have been tiny—the sick feeling of seeing the dead body of a little bird that had just been born. It was near some steps—just pink skin and no feathers.

But I had the most idyllic childhood in England. I really grew up in Kent on my godfather's estate, where my parents had a house. There were hundreds of acres to roam over and a farm of sorts. My brother and I made pets of all the animals—pet rabbits, pet turtles, pet lambs, pet goats, pet chickens. It was my idea of real bliss. When the adults wanted to eat any chickens, they had to buy them in town because we wouldn't let them kill any of ours. I was a very small three when I was given a pony named, oddly enough, Betty. No relation. The first time I got on her back—wearing a little organdy dress—she bucked me into a patch of stinging nettles. But they made me get right back on, and I hardly got off again till we left England.

When I was three and a half, I was in ballet school and once danced before the then Duchess of York, who brought her daughters, Elizabeth and Margaret Rose. The little ones in their white tutus did the butterfly curtsy in which you bent over, half-sitting, half-standing, with your arms extended to the sides and your fingers fluttering. The heads were supposed to be down, but I peeked up through the curtain of my hair and began casing the joint. I loved it. I wouldn't leave the stage. From the wings the teacher was hissing, "Elizabeth, you must come off." Then I started smiling at the audience and they started giggling and the more they giggled, the more I kept smiling. Finally, they lowered the curtain on me.

It was a marvelous feeling on that stage—the isolation, the hugeness, the feeling of space and no end to space, the lights, the music—and then the applause bringing you back into focus, the noise rattling against your face. That was the only time I was ever on stage until the poetry reading when Richard Burton was doing *Hamlet* in New York. Then the butterfly curtsy was in my stomach.

In 1939, when I was seven, we knew the war was coming. Mother and my dad, who was an art dealer in London, were advised to leave England, so we moved to Pacific Palisades near Hollywood and Dad opened a gallery.

Those years before I started acting were truly happy. But I wanted to be an actress—like my mother, who had been on the stage before she married. I think I was probably born a ham. I was constricted by shyness—I still am—and acting meant I could be at ease behind somebody else's facade. When I was little, I'd always be hiding from strangers behind my nurse's back with the finger in the mouth. But if somebody asked me to dance—well, I'd have danced for hundreds of people if they'd asked me—which of course they did not.

And with my very high imagination I spent most of my time in deliberate daydreams—"Walter Mittying"—which I still do now when I'm putting on make-up or doing my nails. Sometimes I Walter Mitty about what I might have done, should have said. Or I write scenes, cast them with people I know or imaginary ones, and play out the plots as if I were the director.

I remember, right after we moved to California, I went to a school where every kid's father was a producer or director or an actor. One day the teacher had each child stand up and tell what he wanted to be and why. Everybody else wanted to be a doctor or a fireman or a nurse. I said *I* wanted to be an actress. They all howled. I remember that red flush creeping all over me, and standing there in an awful hot island. It was, you know, this poor plain thing wants to be a movie star and isn't that a joke. When the laughter died down, I said, "I don't want to be a movie star; I want to be a serious actress like my mother was." And that gave me a little lift of the shoulder, a tilt of the chin.

At that same school I had my first crush. There was the most beautiful boy —to me, then, like a god. One day we were going down the corridor and he tripped me, then picked me up and said, "Hi, there, beautiful." Oh, you can't imagine. I was in such ecstasy, I went to the girls' room and just sat there dreaming. His name was something like Derek Hansen. Later he changed it to John Derek.

There were little boys who had crushes on *me,* but I always kicked them and belted them. One poor little boy tried to kiss me and, oh, God, did I beat him up.

I guess the first serious thought about my acting came when they were casting *Gone With the Wind.* I would be out with my mother shopping and people would come up and say, "Your daughter looks *so* much like Vivien Leigh! Go to Selznick's studio and have her tested for Vivien Leigh's daughter." Of course, each time I was thrilled. But Mother and Dad decided their daughter was going to have a normal life.

However, in that inbred little community most of their friends had something to do with the film industry. When I was nine, a family friend who was head of Universal Studios talked to my parents about allowing an audition. I did a lot of conning of Mother and Dad, and they let me try it. They felt it was a small studio, like a family, and if being in films was spoiling my childhood, they would take me out. I used to sing, if you can believe it, and the casting director instantly disliked me. I was signed anyway, but only did one film. It was called *Man or Mouse,* and my leading man was named Alfalfa—you know, from Our Gang. We played two brats and, as I remember it, all I did was run around and shoot rubber bands at ladies' bottoms.

By the time I left Universal, we'd moved to Beverly Hills and one of Dad's fellow air-raid wardens was a producer named Sam Marx who was doing a film called *Lassie.* It was almost finished except for perhaps ten scenes. These required a little girl with an English accent. The girl they had cast had grown about a foot since they hired her and now they were in a panic to find a substitute. It was during the war and English accents were hard to come by. Mr. Marx got my father to let me audition. I went down to the studio and pretended to pat an imaginary collie on a bare sound stage. It was a snap for a Walter Mittying dog lover.

That film is notable to me mainly because I met its star, a little boy named Roddy McDowall who is now just about my oldest friend—and really the perfect friend. He makes you feel that you're terribly dear to him and even that maybe you're a dear person. He laughs at your jokes so you feel a bit funnier than you actually are. He makes you feel cherished and important. That's his genius. So many of us look for the bad in people if we're at all shy. Roddy looks for the good. It's like the difference between English and French law. With Roddy you are innocent until proven guilty.

M-G-M had owned *National Velvet* for a long time and every once in a while they'd sort of dust it off. But they either couldn't find somebody of the right size or somebody who rode or somebody with an English accent. They began casting glances in my direction. Well, it was my favorite book, and I really was a marvelous horsewoman. At the age of three I could jump without a saddle. But when I came down to the producer's office, he saw that though I was eleven, I was only as tall as a six-year-old. He measured me on the wall and made a line with a pencil. He said, "I'm sorry, honey, but you're just too short. No one would ever believe that you could get in through the jockey's weighing room. You look like a child." And I said, "Well, I'll grow up."

He laughed and patted me on the head.

But I was absolutely determined. *National Velvet* was really me. I started riding every morning for an hour and a half before school. And there was this place Tip's, where they had a thing called a Farm Breakfast—two hamburger patties, two fried eggs, a great big mound of hashed brown potatoes and after that a whole bunch of dollar pancakes. I used to have two Farm Breakfasts every morning at one sitting. For lunch I'd have steaks and salads, then swim and do exercises to stretch myself.

In three months I'd grown three inches. I went back to see the producer and said, "I did grow." He said, "You do look taller." He still had the little mark by the side of the door, and I had grown three inches. He kept that mark on the wall for years. And I got the part.

Being in films then was like the most magical extension of make-believe. It didn't occur to me that it was a career and that I was working for money. I think *Velvet* is still the most exciting film I've ever done. And at the end, to be given the horse on my thirteenth birthday—well, it was one of *the* moments of my life. He was a splendid animal, grand-sired by Man o' War, and I could jump him six feet bareback. But he was wild. He took a hunk out of the shoulder of the man who tried to train him to play dead for the film. Except for the jockey who did some of the jumps in the National, I was about the only person who could ride him—and bareback with just a rope around his neck. That horse used to follow me around the back lot like a puppy dog. He really was a lunatic. Just for the hell of it he once jumped over an automobile.

At that time kid actors were a vogue, usually with animals. There was Roddy and Margaret O'Brien and Peggy Ann Garner, Butch Jenkins and Dean Stockwell and a lot of others. My brother Howard was about fifteen and a most extraordinarily good-looking boy. Universal wanted him to do a western with a horse. He wanted a jalopy and we both were only getting twenty-five cents a week. My parents told him he'd have to earn the money himself and maybe ought to do the film. He did turn up at the studio—but with his whole head shaved absolutely clean, so that there wouldn't be a prayer of getting the part. No one ever again suggested that he go into films. That made me admire him so much.

I worshiped Howard as a child—and still do. He's my best friend of all and I trust him utterly. He is such a wise, tender, brilliant, different man. He is a nonconformist in the true sense, because he doesn't conform to nonconformity. He's not a beatnik, he's not a bohemian. He's Howard Taylor. He's totally unsuperficial, totally unmaterialistic, the most real person I've ever known. In our kind of world that's like a breath of fresh air. I would love to talk a lot about his life, but I have to be very careful not to inflict my fame on him because he has a wonderful sense of his own privacy.

For example, about five years ago he sold everything he owned, bought about a thirty-five-foot sailboat, put his whole family aboard and sailed to Tahiti. They were gone almost four years. And do I admire his wife! Howard wrote back letters to my parents, which were so extraordinary, so dramatic, so beautifully written—and their adventures were so "Kon-Tikian"—that people tried to talk him into having them published. And he said, "No, they're our experiences and they belong to our family. We don't want to commercialize them." God, how I love him for that.

But it *is* Howard's fault that I've never liked to be called "Liz." Like all big brothers, he used to tease me unmercifully when we were kids, calling me Lizzy the Lizard and Lizzy the Cow. It really got my goat. People like to use Liz, I suppose, because it's kind of a nudging word, implies a nodding acquaintance. It can also sound like the most awful hiss—Lizzzzzz.

To do *National Velvet* I signed a contract with M-G-M—and became their chattel until I did *Cleopatra*. The studio then was still in its super era and was truly a most remarkable machine. L. B. Mayer and M-G-M created stars out of tinsel, cellophane and newspapers. Their tremendous publicity staff built the background, built the personality, built the character. Make-up and wardrobe built the facade, and the story department found something just right for that personality. They even had women's directors and men's directors. But all the stars were born and built and died more or less at the whim of L. B. Mayer, who was an absolute dictator of the studio—

and of a good deal of Hollywood to boot.

If you were not in favor, he could blackball you at all the other studios. I was too young to know why all of a sudden a young woman would be blackballed and never be heard of again. Evidently that casting couch bit really did happen. Of course, I never even heard about it until years later.

When M-G-M seemed for a time to be dying, the death rattle was truly horrendous. The atmosphere around the studio was one of tremendous apple-polishing, and of genuine fear that you could smell. Every once in a while they would have a purge and the heads would roll, left, right and center. All the little people—messenger boys, policemen on the gate—who had been there maybe twenty-four years and eight months, and had four months to go before they got a pension—they knew they might be fired any time so M-G-M could save their pension and keep some executive's salary going.

It was a ruthless business. Dick Hanley, who is now my secretary, served L. B. Mayer devotedly, loyally, and was available twenty-four hours a day. I've never known anybody so giving and unselfish. I know that no matter what happens to me, or to him, we will always be friends. I think we know each other as well as two people can—it's been so long and so much has happened—but nothing can ever be *too* much! Richard and I would trust him with our lives—and indeed we do.

Anyway, after Dick Hanley had worked for him for eleven years Mayer told him to take his first vacation. The day Dick began his vacation, he was told that he would have to pay for it himself because he was fired. He didn't even get two weeks' severance pay, not even a thank you or good-bye. And then, because he couldn't stand the thought of Dick working for anybody else, Mayer prevented him for two years from getting another job in Hollywood. Finally Mike Todd, who wasn't afraid of Mayer, hired Dick.

My first sight of L. B. Mayer was even before I signed with Universal. My parents and I were being taken through M-G-M as tourists by the father of a girl friend of mine. I was terrifically impressed. The lot was so huge—at that time they were doing maybe thirty films at once and it was teeming with life—people dressed up in Greek clothes, people dressed up as cowboys, people dressed up as apes, and real live movie stars. Of course everybody, even the extras, looked like movie stars to me.

My friend's father, who was an M-G-M producer, wanted L. B. Mayer to see me. So he took us into the executive building, which I later learned to call the Iron Lung—you know, the executives tell you just how to breathe. L.B. said something like "I want to hear this little girl sing." My mother and I looked at each other and Mother said, "I'm sorry, but I don't have any music and I don't know how to play the piano." L.B. said, "Just sing the scales." So I did— standing there about two feet tall and with a voice so high I could sustain a couple of notes from the top of the keyboard. Then L.B. went dashing off someplace. As he picked up his hat, he said, "Sign her." I didn't sign, but went to Universal instead, only to end up finally at M-G-M about two years later.

Mayer alarmed me terribly. He looked rather like a gross, thick penguin. He had huge glasses and he had a way of looking at you that made you feel completely squashable. You felt his vitality, but you also felt his enormous arrogance, his ego, his overbearing, driving personality. To know him was to be terrified of him.

Every year the whole studio had to celebrate Mayer's birthday. We would all be assembled on Stage Thirty, which would have a dais and then tables for the peasants, like me. Margaret O'Brien would be on the dais because she was a star. Then the kids—it was a command performance—the kids would have to stand around him and sing "Happy Birthday." We were under contract and we were bloody well told to. Then he'd have a picture taken with a kid on each knee. Big Daddy Mayer, the benevolent white father of M-G-M. And he would always say to the whole assembly, even including the peasants, "You must think of me as your father. You must come to me, any of you, with any of your problems, no matter how slight they might seem to you, because you are all my children." And always, you know, he gave with the full gesture, the open-arm embrace.

But just try to get an appointment. And if you ever got behind the golden doors, you would just have to keep your mouth shut. I think once my mother really believed his spiel. I was then about fourteen, and there had been a rumor that I was to do a film called *Sally in Her Alley*. I was supposed to sing and dance in it, and Mother went up with me to ask Big Daddy if it was true and should I begin to train.

He sat behind his desk, looking at these two insects, and blew up. The sweat sprang out on his face and he turned quite white and he stood up and started to rage and shake the building. He used the most obscene language. He yelled at my mother, "You're so god-damned blankety-blank stupid you wouldn't even know what day of the week it is. Don't try to meddle into my affairs. Don't try to tell me how to make motion pictures. I took you out of the gutter."

I sprang to my feet and said, "Don't you dare to speak to my mother like that. You and your studio can both go to hell!" And I ran out of the room, tears pouring down my face, and smack into Dick Hanley. I cried on Dick's shoulder while Mother stayed in there and waited until L.B. calmed down.

I was frightened. I didn't know whether I'd get into trouble with my parents, whether he was still being rude to my mother, whether I should go back in. I thought for sure you don't tell Louis B. Mayer to go to hell in his own studio. I felt guilty because his yelling didn't justify my being rude to him. Then I was told to go in and apologize to him. My dander went right back up again and I said, "No, he was wrong; I'm not going to apologize to him." I never did apologize, and I wasn't fired. I swore I'd never go back into that office, and I never did.

But I admit that all this time when I was young, M-G-M was a very exciting place to be. I've always loved movie stars, loved movies, loved everything about them except doing them. It was so tremendously thrilling to go into the commissary for lunch. They were all there —Judy Garland, Lana Turner, Spencer Tracy, Hedy Lamarr. And there was the lovely, sweet smell of the pancake make-up the women wore—so much more exciting than the grease paint they use now. Every time Clark Gable walked in I just about dropped my fork. He was the epitome of a movie star—so romantic, such bearing, such friendliness. Years later he used to give me a peck on the cheek, which made me shiver. At that time, during the war, tables were never reserved, and I used to die in hopes that Clark Gable would have to sit at mine. The closest I got, though, was Marjorie Main.

I even used to carry an autograph book, which I was tremendously proud of. One day, when I was about fourteen, Katharine Hepburn was sitting at a table right behind me in the commissary. I went over to her and said, "Excuse me, ma'am, would you mind signing my book?" I guess I must have interrupted her in the middle of something because when she took my autograph book, it was as though she didn't even see me. I guess because I was in such awe of her—she was one of the really golden ones—all of a sudden I got ice cold and white hot and started shaking. She was perfectly nice, but that was the last autograph I ever asked for.

There were two other girls on the block where I lived and we called ourselves the Three Musketeers.

When I'd come home from the studio —I'd get out at twelve, have lunch in the commissary and then have singing lessons, so I'd get home around three— then we'd play. Of course, like most little girls we were very romantic and all had our own imaginary boy friends. We'd make up plays for ourselves and make up stories, and of course I was really *in*, because I could say, "Well, I know Van Johnson, so Van Johnson is going to be *my* boy friend today. But I'll let *you* have him tomorrow."

God! That seems so long ago, so sweet, so clean.

CHAPTER TWO

THE DAY CAME, of course, when I got a bit famous. I still wanted to be part of the lives of my girl friends on the block, but it was not possible. I think they began to regard me as a sort of oddity. And any carefree privacy had pretty much disappeared under the constant chaperoning, constant surveillance, constant work. It was always, "Don't chew your cud too loudly, be on your best behavior"—all part of the simple fact that I was rapidly becoming worth a lot of money to a lot of people.

Not being like other children, not belonging to the adult world and not belonging to a children's world, I felt always the outsider. Even the film kids were not really in my mold. Their parents were always giving parties so that the movie magazines like *Photoplay* or

Movie Gems could come and photograph their children. They had swimming-pool parties or let's-paint-your-fence parties, and so on. I usually would have a ball when I would go—swimming without a swimming cap, coming up from too deep a dive and regurgitating water—all the things you shouldn't do if you wanted to be photographed. But then I'd look around. I'd see that most everybody else—even the kids—were performing almost entirely for the camera. I'd feel absolutely lost.

I did a lot of reading, painting, drawing in those days—anything that was escapism, I suppose. I went to the movies all the time. Horseback riding meant everything to me—the friendly isolation, the solitude, the companionship with the animal. It was a marvelously therapeutic thing. My mother was my best girl friend, my guide, my mentor, my constant companion. I told her every kind of inside fear I had.

It was then that I began acquiring my dislike of press agents. The people in the M-G-M press department would suggest that I date somebody, and I would immediately rebel. Nobody was going to decide for me whom to date, what to wear,

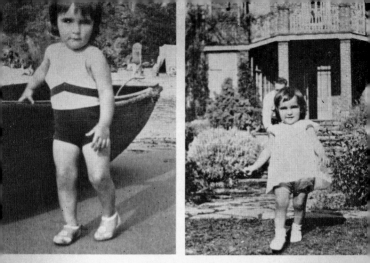

Seeing these pictures again of herself at age 2—on a beach in England, and right, at her family's house in High Gate—Elizabeth Taylor exclaimed, "What a pudge!"

At four, Elizabeth Taylor poses in a party dress, and right, with her father, Francis Taylor.

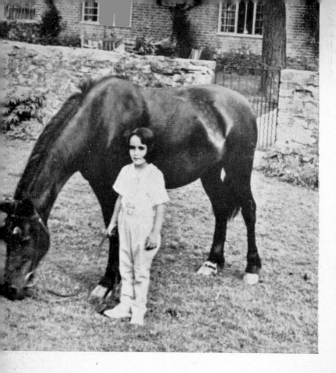

Above, on her grandfather's estate in Kent, she is a diminutive six beside her horse, Betty. Below left, she is with her brother Howard, age 11. Recollecting the dog's name—Spot—she said, "What an *original* name!" At age 10 she sits, below right, for a publicity still for the film which launched her: *Lassie*, starring the original Lassie and Roddy McDowall, still a close friend.

A price of Elizabeth Taylor's fame and glamour—epitomized by the sitting for photographer Richard Avedon on the previous page—is the mob of fans which throngs to get a glimpse of her and Richard Burton wherever they go. During his *Hamlet* in New York, thousands gathered nightly.

At the stage door, a phenomenon which has never been matched on Broadway. Then, as the Burtons drove away, the fans would surge forward, as in the sequence above, to peer into the limousine. When the car had passed, people would turn to each other exclaiming, "I saw them!"

For Elizabeth Taylor, fame carries with it serious business decisions with her lawyer and friend, Aaron Frosch—above—at the ever-present fan, below left, who pops out of nowhere with a camera "Please, Miss Taylor, just one shot." And then there is, right, the inevitable photograph to be signed.

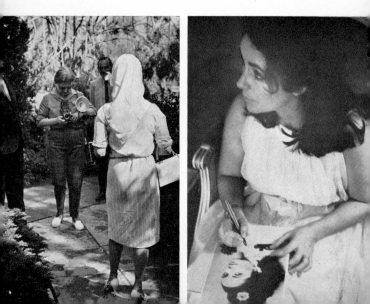

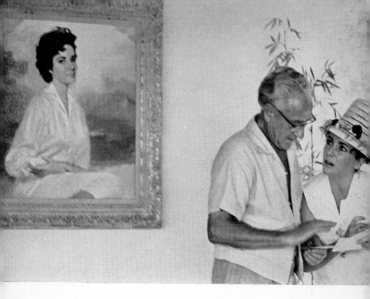

With her father, above, she looks at childhood snapshots. At
bottom left, an art dealer, gives his famous son-in-law a brief lec-
ture on painting. At right, spending a day with her parents in
Beverly Hills, Elizabeth Taylor, always an eager eater, picks a
piece of chicken.

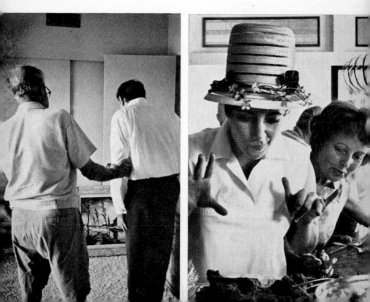

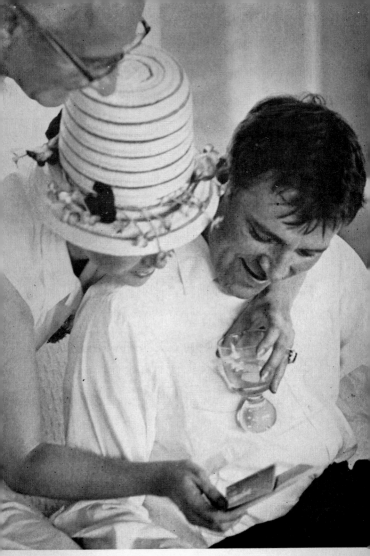

With her father, Elizabeth Taylor shows to an amused Richard Burton some of the childhood pictures which appear early in this book. She remembers those days in England as "the most idyllic childhood."

or put words in my mouth. I was either going to make a fool of myself or not, but it was going to be *me*.

I didn't date until I was about sixteen —and then it was with boys of twenty-three. With kids my own age I was gawky and terrified. To them I was a freak—"you know, Howard Taylor's kid sister who is in films." I was never invited to football games, or basketball games at the school where the girls on my block went. I was never invited to proms, except once when I went with a friend of Howard's and had a perfectly miserable time.

I felt so out of place. I knew nothing about sports. I didn't even know about exams, because I always had to go down to the Board of Education to be tested. It was almost as though they deliberately chose to talk about their inside goings-on to make it quite clear that I was not one of them. Well, it worked!

I hated my own school because it wasn't school. The M-G-M classroom was in what used to be Irving Thalberg's bungalow, and I went there from the age of ten until I graduated. We were required by law to put in three hours a day, so we were doing in that time what normal kids did in six. During a film you'd have a special tutor on the set. So between camera takes you'd cram in ten minutes, twenty minutes of study—going out to act, then being led by the ear back to school and snapping your brain back into being a student.

My brother used to tell me what it was like to go to school. And I thought, how marvelous, just to be able even to cheat, to look over somebody's shoulder. But I never had anybody else's shoulder to look over. There were never more than a half-dozen or so of us in the studio school, and everybody else was always in a different grade.

We were under constant supervision. If you happened to look up at the ceiling, even if you were thinking about the book you were reading, you would have your knuckles rapped, verbally. Eyes back to the book! and I imagine that kids in real school, if the teacher reprimands them, exchange conspiratorial looks with their chums and snigger. Well, there was not even a chance for that.

I was in constant rebellion. I used to try to escape by going into the bathroom and Walter Mittying—until the teacher finally caught on to me. I had come back out after ten minutes or so, and in front of the whole class I was reprimanded. After that, when I legitimately had to go to the bathroom, I would write on the blackboard, in very small letters: "E enters bathroom 10:03," then: "E exits bathroom 10:06, mission accomplished." Finally, in due course, I was reprimanded for that, as indeed I should have been.

In spite of all this, I really had pretty good grades—A's and B's—I guess because I have a photographic memory. Today I can learn several pages of a script just by reading them over a few times. Just before an exam I would memorize the points I thought they would ask me about. Of course, two weeks later it was gone, so I really didn't absorb anything in my so-called education. And I knew, even then, that I was cheating myself.

My graduation was the only day I've ever set foot in a real high school. After you graduate from the Board of Education you are told the name of a high school to go to. You put on a cap and gown, and you stand in line alphabetically with all the students who have gone to this school and have been chums together for four years. And you are given a diploma—you graduate—and you get out of there as quickly as you can. You don't know one single soul. You really feel a bit of a crumpet—like you're acting a ruddy scene in a cap and gown.

The principal of the high school I was sent to started talking about how some of us that day were going out into the world to try to find jobs and how others of us would go on to college and then go out and seek a way of life and a livelihood—and how some of us would have difficulty finding a living. But we must persevere and what the school had given us would be the foundation of our lives.

Well, at that time I was making something like two thousand dollars a week, and had been working since I was ten years old. I started to get the giggles. All kinds of perverse thoughts were going through my mind and at the same time I felt like such a fool and intruder. It was uncontrollable, like giggling in church. And the giggle evidently was contagious. The girl in front of me started to giggle, then someone in the back. And then, all around the hall, there was this awful rustle. It was just like mice—or chipmunks—nibbling away at the structure of stability this man was talking about.

By that time I was seventeen and I wanted desperately to go to college and get a real education. But I just didn't think I could stand being treated like a freak. The other means of running away was marriage.

I was, I am afraid, wildly infatuated with love. At the age of sixteen—when I looked about twenty-four—I was playing Robert Taylor's wife in *Conspirator*. I'd finish a passionate love scene with him and then the tutor would drag me away to study mathematics. I mean it really kind of made your eyes go crossed!

And I'd barely, by then, received my first real-life kiss—a smack and a dart into the house—the boy was Marshal Thompson, a young actor. I was terrified before my first screen kiss in *Cynthia*, but my second screen kiss was a "breeze." It was with Peter Lawford in *Julia Misbehaves*. Peter to me was the last word in sophistication. He was terribly handsome, and I had a tremendous crush on him. He invited me out twice after shooting, but he never did kiss me in private life. I was so thrilled that he had taken me out, because I was only sixteen and felt about twelve. The *whole* company knew I had a crush on him. In the scene where he had to kiss me I was supposed to say, "Oh, Rock, what are we going to do?" After the kiss I looked at him, turned a hot scarlet and said, "Oh, Peter, what am I going to do?" And the whole company fell down laughing. That's another moment when you want the floor to open.

The press had me going steady with Glenn Davis because I wore his gold football around my neck while he was in Korea seven months. It was so childish; two sweet children. I remember reading the papers at the time and I thought, My God, they think it's a big hot romance!

I wore Bill Pawley's ring for a few months, but that was equally childish. We went well together under the palm trees; we looked nice on the dance floor; we loved to go boating; we had nothing in common in our lives.

I really thought in those days that just because I became a Mrs. instead of a Miss, just because I hit twenty-one, something would automatically happen to me inside. I was always wanting to be older, always trying the superficial things of being sophisticated. I don't think I even analyzed whether it was maturity I wanted—probably just the glamour of being a woman.

I did have moments of self-revelation. When I was sixteen, I said something about being an emotional child inside a woman's body and the press picked it up. I recently have read that it's a shame I didn't say it, that it came out of a press agent's mouth. You want to meet whoever said that and give him a knuckle sandwich.

I had always had a very strict and proper upbringing—and absolutely necessary it was, living the existence I did. The irony is that the morality I learned at home required marriage, I couldn't just have an affair. So I got married all those times, and now I'm accused of being a scarlet woman. I guess I never gave myself the time to find out whether a thing was love or infatuation. I always chose to think I was in love. I didn't know. I didn't have my own yardstick. But I did believe that love was synonymous with marriage.

So I got engaged—to Nick Hilton—at barely eighteen. I really did think that being married would be like living in a little white cottage with a little picket fence and little roses and little me in an organdy apron.

Nick, of course, was a Roman Catholic, and after taking my instructions I had to sign a paper saying that I was ready and willing to bear children. Well, I knew that I was a terribly immature girl. I was dying to have children, but I wanted at least a year of marriage to become responsible for myself before I could attempt the responsibility of being a good mother.

I explained all that to the priest and finally ended up with an archbishop, explaining again that I wanted to be a good wife and a splendid mother, but that I was so inexperienced and thought I needed a bit of time. Well, that doesn't "go" with the Church. This was about two weeks before the wedding—the invitations, everything, had been sent out. The archbishop said that unless I signed the paper I could not be married in the Church. And I said, "Well, I'll have to think about it because it's a matter of swearing before God." Finally I did sign the paper.

The ceremony was like a fairy tale. It was perfect. I was terrified. So was Nick

—I remember taking out my handkerchief and mopping the sweat off his face during the ceremony. There was a big reception and, for the first time in my life, I had two glasses of champagne. Then the time came to leave and I had a third glass of champagne. And I became more and more afraid. My bridesmaids dragged me off and stuffed me into my going-away suit. I wanted to run. I was so scared. I really had no idea what was coming.

The honeymoon in Europe lasted two weeks. I should say the marriage lasted for two weeks. Then came, yours sincerely, disillusionment—rude and brutal.

There's nothing more to be said about that first marriage. It scarred me and left me with horrible memories. I am sure this was also true for Nick. But the marriage has nothing to do with my life now; I have no children by him. He's not part of my life and I'm no part of his life.

Marrying Nick had been so easy, so like a fairy tale. Everything was lovely; my parents, everyone approved—too perfect, too picturesque, too ideal. When I left him, it was to be the first divorce in our family, and I was totally crushed. I was afraid of sympathy or understanding from anybody. I was afraid of myself. I was afraid to go back to Nick. I was afraid of my total failure. I was afraid of the disappointment to my parents and his parents. I was afraid to be alone. I guess I was afraid of growing up.

But I didn't go home, back to the warm nest. I moved into an apartment with my stand-in—trying to stand on my own and *not* be afraid! My parents were always loving and understanding and didn't hold the separation against me. They were always there to be called upon, like a fountain to be tapped. But they realized that I was going through a tremendous growing-up agony, and that I simply had to try by myself to understand myself—where I had gone wrong. At the age of eighteen I got ulcers and was living close to a nervous breakdown, but divorcing Nick was the first grown-up decision I ever made absolutely alone.

I understood finally just how much I had been living on a cotton-candy cloud. And now that reality had finally hit me and I'd fallen off, I didn't have any of the protection of normal growth. I refused to fall back on anybody but myself—and there was nothing there to fall back on. It was pretty lonely. All day, every day, there had been somebody right there to rely on. Why, when I was seventeen and wanted to visit another set to see a friend, I had to get permission from the social worker-tutor. It was the law. I wasn't even supposed to go to the commissary alone. And there was almost never a moment to be alone, to reflect, to think, be silent, just be by myself.

When I kicked myself out of the nest and got married, I had been vaguely aware that I ought to have been more self-sufficient. But it really cracked home when I realized I had been a virgin not only physically but mentally. I mean, I didn't know *anything*—like cooking a meal, like not being sloppy, not throwing your clothes on the floor and expecting somebody else to hang them up. I didn't like to give orders to servants—it made me feel funny—but I was incapable of doing anything for myself or for other people. At the first sign of trouble between Nick and me I didn't have one clue how to cope with it.

When I divorced Nick, I said on the witness stand that he had told me to go to hell, and insulted my mother and insulted me in front of friends. That was absolutely the smallest, weakest grounds possible, and the only ones I would allow my lawyers to go into. I could have gone into such a multitude of really horrendous things to make what I was doing understandable. But I didn't want anything from Nick. I didn't want alimony. I certainly didn't want to hurt him. I didn't want to be the wronged woman. The hurt that had happened was too private. Ever since I'd been twelve, I'd been a child star with no privacy, and very possessive about my own thoughts and problems. Until the separation I told practically nobody that there were problems, to say nothing of the nature of the problems.

CHAPTER THREE

WHEN YOU ARE YOUNG and you fall off your cloud for the first time, you try to make yourself believe everything is still beautiful. After my divorce from Nick, I worked very hard at this—perhaps too hard. My career gave me something to do. And I had some wonderful chums who made me feel loved but weren't always trying to get serious.

Montgomery Clift and Roddy McDowall made possible the first spree I'd ever had in my life. I had been to Europe to do a piece of cachou called *Ivanhoe* and had needed a combination chaperone, secretary and "nursemaid" to look after me. Now, back in New York, alone and independent for the very first time, I moved into the Plaza Hotel and was given a sumptuous suite. I was on my own expenses so I called down to find out the daily rate. They said, "Not at all, Miss Taylor. It's with the compliments of the house." I said, "Oh, really? How nice." And I stayed for six weeks.

All I did was have fun doing crazy things with my chums—staying up as late as I wished. If I had a whim to go ice skating at nine o'clock at night, there was always somebody to say, "Come on, let's do it!" Or we'd go feed animals in the zoo or feed ourselves nothing but hot dogs all day long—completely irresponsible sort of behavior. I didn't have to eat properly. I didn't have to keep proper hours. I had a ball.

The day came when I thought I'd better get my bill—for food and stuff. It was $2,500. My "complimentary" stay at the hotel had been for four days. I almost died. I decided to stay in one room at the St. Regis, where my uncle lived. Roddy and Monty came and helped me pack.

Somebody that day had sent me six dozen double chrysanthemums—those things you wear at football games. And I'm afraid we ordered about a bowl of martinis while we were packing. We got into a chrysanthemum fight, dueling—*en garde, touche*. The petals fell, like fall leaves, all over everything, and while I was packing, the boys hung all the paintings upside down.

When I got to the St. Regis and unpacked my bag, I found a shower nozzle in my suitcase—and all the Plaza Hotel towels, bathmats, everything—even the martini carafe. That was the work of my dear old friend, Monty. But then we felt terribly remorseful.

I called the head housekeeper to apologize. On the telephone I said, "May I have the head housekeeper for the sixth floor, please?" And I waited for ages. "But we can't find the head housekeeper on the sixth floor, we don't know where she is." I said, "Well, could you find me any head housekeeper, please?" "Well, they all seem to have disappeared." "Well, could you find me one of the maids or one of the waiters on the sixth floor, please?" They said, "Well, it's a curious thing, they all seem to have disappeared." I said, "Well, why don't you try ringing room such-and-such"—my suite. They rang and when somebody answered, it sounded like a convention going on. They were *all* in there. And I apologized like mad and sent flowers and perfume and candy to everyone.

I was reveling in being free—out of my incubator—when along came one of those very nasty realities of fame that the studio and my parents had always shielded me from. I got some obscene bomb-threat letters through the mail, and then by telephone. Eventually, so that the police could have time to trace the call, I had to keep this maniac on the phone for half an hour by listening to disgusting descriptions of what he was going to do to me.

This came on top of something that happened in the South of France so terrifying and so spooky that I was still haunted by it. I had gone down there with my secretary-companion on a holiday from *Ivanhoe* and hoped to get a little calm with some friends, Bob and Sue Douglas. We flew from London in an eight-passenger, two-engine plane. You know that funny feeling that two eyes are boring into the back of your head? On this little plane I had that feeling, but every time I whirled around nobody was looking.

Bob and Sue met us and said, "Oh, darlings, have a glass of champagne." In the airport bar this rather distinguished-looking gentleman came up. He had a mustache and was very well tailored. He said, "May I buy you and your party another bottle of champagne?" We said, "No, but thank you very much." He said, "Oh, but I insist." And I said, "Well, thank you, but we are leaving in a minute." He said, "You don't know who I am, do you?" "Well, no," I said. "I'm awful at names." And he said, "Well, I feel you owe me the privilege of buying you a bottle of champagne." The man had become so persistent that Bob finally said, "Okay, fine, old man, thanks, thank you terribly, a tiny little split will do, thank you." Then the stranger left, still looking at me in the funniest kind of smirking way. He got into an Italian sports car, one of the lowest, raciest kinds.

That night we all went to the casino. And the same man was there, and no matter what table we stopped at, he followed. When we went back to the boarding-house-hotel, that big sports car followed us. The next morning we all went downstairs about seven-thirty to a sidewalk cafe where we had breakfast. And this chap just walked up and down, nodding at us but saying nothing—no indication, no clue, nothing. Then we went swimming. And the fellow was there on the beach.

Bob and I got caught in a treacherous ebb tide, and we almost drowned. We were walking on a long sandbar through water up to our waists and were talking very intently. All of a sudden the sandbar dropped out from under us and the tide was so swift we were really almost drowned. It was terrifying. We straggled back to the hotel and there was the man again, staring silently. We had dinner at the hotel, and the man had his dinner at a table nearby.

The next morning, I slept late and I met everybody downstairs about nine-thirty. Bob said, "That funny chap handed me an envelope to give you." The letter said: "Dear Miss Taylor, quite clearly you do not remember me. I am the man you had thrown in jail for six months and deported from the United States of America. I think you owe me something and I intend to collect."

My heart went "thunk"—and I told my friends what had happened.

When I was just about seventeen, the studio received some obscene letters addressed to me. The writer threatened to murder me and to do all kinds of other things before murdering me. For about three months I was trailed by the cops and the FBI. My parents were even told at one point that we should carry a gun in the glove compartment of the car. God, can you imagine how excited I was! Carrying a gun! And maybe even a pearl-handled one! Of course, Mother and Dad said no.

Finally, the police caught a man climbing over the back wall of our garden in Beverly Hills. He had a room in a cheap motel, and in the room they found maps with detailed time charts of exactly where I had gone and with whom, day after day, from sunup to evening. They put him in jail for six months, and then deported him back to England where he had come from.

I got all the details from my friend Ed, the policeman who caught him. And I said, "What was he like? What did he look like? Can I go to the trial?" I wasn't allowed to, of course.

Now here he was in the South of France—and probably had been one of those eight passengers on that plane. I said to Bob, "What are we going to do? What does he mean?" And Bob said,

"Well, I don't know, it just sounds like he's trying to frighten you." "Well, you want to know something?" I said. "He *has* frightened me."

We left that afternoon, and I have never heard from the man since.

All this time my efforts to climb back on my cloud were failing. I was still on a treadmill, breathlessly running too fast—full of panic, fear, self-doubts. I was floundering, doing impulsive things, not caring whether I was heading for disaster, letting myself get swept along.

I thought Michael Wilding, twenty years older than I, was sort of an island, an oasis, and indeed he was. He restored all sanity and, at age twenty, I married him. He represented tranquillity, security, maturity—all the things I needed in myself. But I found that unfortunately you can't get them just by touching somebody else.

We had a lovely, easy life, very simple, very quiet. Two babies were born. We had friends. We didn't do much. We'd sit around the pool, play with our babies. We raised cats and dogs, read a lot, fought with kindhearted old M-G-M and worried about money problems.

Michael was—and is—a marvelous companion, very witty and a wonderful raconteur. We had our own sort of language, and he used to break up over my American slang and I over his Briticisms. And he'd be so stoically British! When I was in a real fury, my biggest oath, the worst thing I could say to him—and it always amused him vastly—was "You're such a goddamn Englishman!"

It's very difficult for me to remember what it was like to be married to Michael Wilding. In fact, sometimes it is very difficult to believe that we were *ever* married. I can't visualize the emotion of a lover other than the love I have for him now—which is totally different. It's so utterly platonic on both sides. He's just one of the people dearest to me in the whole world.

I had gone, before we were married, to a top doctor in New York who told me that I could conceive, but would always after a few months have miscarriages unless I came to him three days a week for a year and got certain shots. It was a fantastic blow; I was dying to have children. But I was nineteen and thought *"Noblesse oblige,"* so I went to Michael full of tears and said, "I don't think you'd

better marry me; I can't have children."
Michael was very comforting and insisted he was marrying me for me. Well, that doctor was a lying quack. In three months I was pregnant with little Michael.

I was absolutely idiotic with pride. You would have thought I was the only woman who had ever conceived and carried a child. I was doing a film until I was five months pregnant, and the baby didn't show at all. I was wearing with ease dresses twenty-three inches around the waist. But the day I finished the film, I rushed out and bought my maternity wardrobe. I immediately began waddling around with the feet turning in and my stomach stuck out ahead of me till I looked like a sway-backed old horse. And when I'd sit down, I'd give out the big sigh of relief that pregnant women do. And all the time there was only like a little thimble under my shirt. To get fat in the stomach I began indulging in all my pregnant whims and was delighted when I got up to a hundred and fifty pounds. And the bigger I got, the more benign and happy I got, like a big momma. And I still went around sticking out my stomach. I was so proud.

I don't think there's any feeling quite like a baby's kick inside your stomach. I used to send SOS's all around the house, to the cook, to the gardener—"The baby's kicking." When you have to get up in the dark at night, you instinctively and without knowing it walk with your hands in front of your stomach to protect the little thing inside you. I went through the same cataclysm again with Christopher two years later.

Oh, I wish I could completely explain how I feel about having a baby. It's that procreation is the greatest miracle of all, and you are participating in it, contributing to it—as animals must do, as the grizzly bears must do because they kill to protect their cubs. You feel an affinity with all the vast things in the world since time began. And you feel so small. Procreation is like the tide, it's like the planets, it's like everything inexplicable. And yet it's so utterly personal. And the baby is so tiny, so vulnerable, everything is so tentative. Because you're such a crucial part of such a miracle, I think every mother when she's carrying a baby must feel tremendously important. I know I've never felt so important in my life. I've never felt so beautiful.

When I was pregnant with Christopher, Michael Wilding and I began looking for a larger house and we came across a house high on a hilltop with a "for sale" sign on it. The architect was a man called George MacLean whom I'd always admired. We walked around the outside and peered at it, and then I got brave and we climbed over the wall and trespassed.

A workman had left a glass sliding door open and we went inside. The whole place was completely carpeted and had running water and somebody had left behind a bottle of sherry, and there were paper cups and we sat on the floor, looked at the view, and there was a record machine so we put records on. We drank the sherry and sat there for a couple of hours and fell in love with the house—explored every inch of it.

It was indoors and outdoors all at the same time—the outdoors brought inside. One whole wall was built of bark with fern and orchids growing up the bark, and the bar was made of stone. And the fireplace had no chimney. There was a device making the smoke go down under the building and out through the barbecue pit. So it was like a Walt Disney

Snow White setting. You really couldn't distinguish between the outside and inside. And all the colors I loved—off white, white, natural woods, stone, beigy marble. The pool was so beautiful. There were palm trees and rock formations—it looked like a natural pool, with trees growing out of it. It was the most beautiful house I've ever seen.

We later took picnics to the house and then it just seemed to belong to us. We knew that somehow or other we had to buy it. But we knew it would be way too expensive for us. We'd never met George MacLean, only heard of him, but we called him and confessed what we'd done. He laughed and said that he would like to meet us. In the meantime, we told my mother and dad what we'd done and about the house. Mother said George MacLean's first wife had been an old friend of hers, and she had said that George always had to have some kind of focal point, some image or a person to build a house for. Sometimes they were people he'd never met. Then Mother said, "Didn't you know? He built that house for you, Elizabeth."

That clinched it. We bought it for $150,000 and went way into debt.

George became a great friend and god-father to Christopher.

I guess our life *had* to be quiet in those years because we were always worried about going broke. Every time I got pregnant, kindhearted old M-G-M would put me on suspension.

It was about this time in my life that I began my really ludicrous series of accidents—and there have been too many to be believed. We were doing the stills for *Elephant Walk* and Peter Finch, Dana Andrews and I had to look like we were driving a jeep with the wind blowing in our hair. They had an airplane propeller trained on us. Evidently the wind picked a tiny piece of metal up from the floor and as we were throwing our heads back against the wind something hit my eye. Every time I blinked, there would be the most awful scratching sensation. Later, when the eye got goopy and stuff was coming out, I went to a doctor who probed around and said, "My dear, you have a foreign object in your eye." And I said, "Anybody I know?" Another doctor put my head in a little vise and operated to get out my foreign object. It had shot deep into the eyeball and had rusted. They can't knock you out because you have to keep your eye open and stare at a certain spot on the wall. They have a needle with a tiny knife at the end and you can hear them cutting your eye. It sounds rather like eating watermelon on a minor scale.

When he finished, he bandaged my eye up and said, "You really must be terribly careful because we don't want the fluid to leave your eye, do we?" And I said, "No, indeed we don't. What would happen if it did?" And he said, "Well, your eye would look rather like a dried-up raisin." And I said, "Oh, no, indeed, we *do* want to keep our fluid."

A couple of days later—it was my first Mother's Day—I was playing with my baby when he went pow with his little fist and cracked me right in the eye. The pain was excruciating and I felt some wet stuff on my cheek underneath the bandage so I called the doctor. He took the bandage off and said, "Oh, my God." An ulcer had formed, completely covering the eye.

This time they operated at the hospital—and, strangely enough, injected me with typhoid fever. As I understand it, an induced fever stimulates one's overall resistance to infection. Both eyes were bandaged and it was two weeks before I would find out whether I would lose that eye.

It was weird not being able to see. The bed had bars up the sides so I wouldn't fall out, but in two days I knew where to reach everything through the bars—where to turn the radio on, where my perfume was, the cold cream, the glass of water. I was terribly proud and not too depressed working on my little accomplishments. When Michael came to see me I said, "Hey, how about this?" And I reached out, showing off like mad, and knocked over the bottle of perfume. That was the first time I cried. That silly little thing made me snap.

It's strange, but I didn't worry too much then—or during any of my illnesses—whether my career would be ended. By then it was only a way of making money. It was very hard to take any great interest in a career of playing the perennial ingenue—an appeal to bobby-soxers, to people who read movie magazines—always the same part with a happy ending.

The films I did then have sort of blanked out in my mind, because they were so distasteful to me. There was

Conspirator, which I hope not many people have seen. Even *Ivanhoe* was just a big medieval western. A lot of them I haven't seen, but I must have been appalling in them. I did enjoy doing *The Last Time I Saw Paris,* even though it wasn't supposed to be a good film. God, when I think of some of the movies, like *Beau Brummell*. I never saw that film until after Richard and I were married. It was on television and Richard turned it on. I had to change stations after about five minutes—I mean *I* was so embarrassing in it.

All I did was just sort of whistle and hum my way through those films, powdering my nose and getting a great kick out of wearing pretty clothes—dying to wear more make-up, higher heels, lower-cut dresses. The first time I ever considered *acting* when I was young was in *A Place in the Sun*. I was seventeen and thrilled to be in the film because it was my first kind of adult role. It was a tricky part, because the girl is so rich and spoiled that it would have been easy to play her as absolutely vacuous. But I think she was a girl who could care a great deal.

That was when I first met Montgomery Clift, who ever since then has been practically my dearest friend. But that day in the director's office I had the full scale of teen-age palpitations. I thought he was the most gorgeous thing in the world and easily one of the best actors. But in a pair of jeans, slouched in a chair, he was hardly the austere, mysterious, affected, Method Studio actor I was expecting. And he wasn't a bit snide about acting with a "cheap movie star."

I remember thinking, Here I am, working with Montgomery Clift, a genu-ine stage actor. Naturally I didn't know what Method meant, but it sounded serious. So I thought, I'm going to be serious too, by God! He had a coach and I didn't understand that because I had never even had acting lessons, much less a coach. Then the little ego began working away and I began thinking, Well, Method! They evidently sort of work themselves into a thing by transplanting themselves out of reality and making the fiction reality. And I watched Monty. I watched how much time he spent on concentration—which has since become the key to my kind of acting, if you can call it acting.

Monty is the most emotional actor I

have ever worked with. And it is contagious. When he would start to shake, I would start to shake. Only two actors I know, Monty and Richard, give to the degree that it's almost a physical thing, like an umbilical cord, an electricity that goes back and forth.

I did *A Place in the Sun* on loan to Paramount, and tried hard in it. I felt I had done well and now maybe M-G-M would give me a break. It gave me a bit of heart, which was soon lost again—lost under a morass of mediocrity. Not just the scripts. I was mediocre, too.

My next big opportunity didn't come until I was married to Michael Wilding and heard about *Giant,* which was going to be done by Warner Brothers. The role I wanted started at the age of eighteen and ended up a very pedicured, manicured, well-coifed, well-dressed fifty. And that is about the most difficult age to portray if you are twenty-two, as I was.

George Stevens' first choice was Grace Kelly, but they couldn't get her, and M-G-M didn't want to let me go. So I had to stamp my flat feet for quite a while in the iron lung, pleading to be given a chance to do a film I considered good. I had to go almost on a sit-down strike. Of course I realized Grace Kelly was a lot more desirable actress, a much "hotter actress," than I was. All I wanted was a chance for seconds. But M-G-M wanted me for some other film—like a sequel to Lassie's mother, or something. Anyway, finally they couldn't get Grace Kelly, and George settled on me. I got no extra money for it. M-G-M got the money. It was just a chance to do a part that was an opportunity and with a director like George.

George has made some great movies. His law of averages is marvelous. He was my director in *A Place in the Sun*. I really had a case of hero worship for him then, and desperately wanted to please. When I did *A Place in the Sun*, I was still a minor. I was protected by a social worker and could only work so many hours. No one was allowed to swear on the set. George couldn't have treated me more wonderfully. I found out on *Giant*, however, that he tends to like having a patsy or two on a film. Jimmy Dean was one and I was another, but I'll say this for George—he usually picks people who *can* answer back.

At the same time, he had a kind of

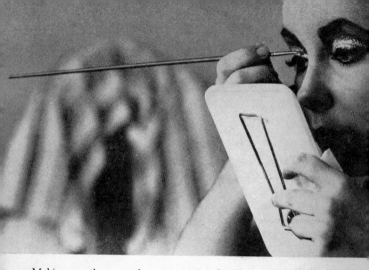

Making up the most famous eyes in the film world, Elizabeth Taylor paints on gold for her *Cleopatra* role, and, below, does her eyes for *The Sandpiper*. She was born with a double row of eyelashes, but insists her eyes are not violet as publicized and are different colors depending on what she wears.

A habitual mugger, Elizabeth Taylor poses demurely for Roddy McDowall on the *Cleopatra* set, above left, and then, below left, she gets bored with being serious and begins hamming with a "So what's new?" gesture. Above, after a party for Liza, she gasps, "Thank God!" and sprawls out in mock collapse. "Poor Roddy," she once said happily, "I've ruined so much of his film."

Two classic Elizabeth Taylors are the incorrigible clown and the tender beauty. At left is a gallery of grotesques collected by Mc-Dowall over a period of years. Above, on the set of *The Sandpiper* she gently strokes a sandpiper and makes friends with it so that the little bird will fly back and perch on her shoulder on cue. She succeeded.

Playing with her parrot at her Puerto Vallarta house in Mexico, Elizabeth Taylor, at top left, lets the bird peck at her lips as Michael watches fascinated. Then, bottom left, she gives it a bath under a running tap. Below, she cuddles her nephew Layton Taylor. She is extremely close to her brother, Howard, who has always been very careful to keep his family and himself out of the glare of publicity and gossip focused on his sister.

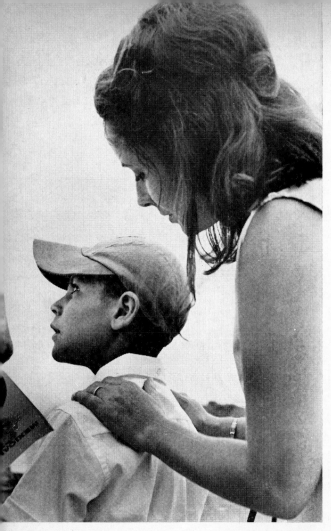

In Mexico Elizabeth Taylor sees off on an airplane a little boy whom she and Richard Burton were sending to an eye surgeon in Guadalajara. Suffering from an advanced cataract in one eye, he was a bootblack who shined Richard Burton's shoes every day during the filming of *Night of the Iguana*. The eye turned out to be past saving, but, says Elizabeth Taylor, "He did get a chance to go to about ten movies."

love for Jimmy Dean. It was curious to watch him. They'd meet head on and there'd be a terrible clash. Then, when I was not on camera, I would watch George watching Jimmy. George would smile, but he didn't ever let Jimmy know that he was fond of him. Rock Hudson he wanted to manipulate, and Rock proved, I think, that he *could* really act. He had never done a serious film, and had been considered a beautiful man per se—a subject for movie magazines. I don't think George likes opposition. I think he prefers clay.

Shooting the film turned out to be murderous. A fight over costumes, for instance. When the girl goes back to Virginia after leaving her husband, George wanted me to look desperate and sad and lonely, and he put me in a costume of thick brogue shoes, thick stockings, a long skirt, a man's slouch hat and my hair in a tight bun. I felt like a damn fool and worse. I couldn't see why the girl, an utterly feminine woman, would deliberately put on a ludicrous getup that made her look a lesbian in drag—or Charlie Chaplin. I told George this.

In front of the whole crew, in a very large voice, he announced that all I cared about was how I looked, and quite clearly I would never become an actress because I was so concerned about being glamorous. So to prove I didn't care what I looked like, I wiped all the make-up off my face, and without a mirror I loosened my hair and just yanked it back, twisted it like the two strands of a braid, and fastened it with a rubber band. There was a whole huge battle. I think I got rid of the hat. Nobody won, nobody lost; we did the scene. It was like that during the whole film.

I had trouble with my back and George was quite convinced it was all psychosomatic. But it is a characteristic of sciatica that it's crippling one moment and disappears the next. Much later, after my back operation, Mike Todd wanted to send him the X-rays of my spine for a Christmas card.

On one day there was a scene after she—the girl I played—had separated from her husband. Her younger sister is getting married and she is the matron of honor. During the ceremony the estranged husband, played by Rock Hudson, comes through the door and edges up in back of me. As the marriage vows are said, I was to turn and see Rock. It's as if the wedding vows are being said again for us and, naturally, the two go back together again. The whole thing is done with just eyes and looks—a fairly obvious piece of acting.

Now we were all in our costumes; we'd done rehearsals umpteen times and broken for lunch. I came back from lunch and my dress had to be pressed and I was sitting in my very large dressing room on the set waiting to be called. Something like an hour went by. They had called the extras on, there were about seventy-five of them, and I thought, Well, they're rehearsing the extras. My make-up man and the hairdresser were sitting in the room with me and we kept saying, "What the hell are they doing? My God, it's been hours."

So finally I thought, Well, I'll go out and see what's going on, and I walked onto the set. All the lights had been turned off. The extras were all standing there. George was sitting in his director's chair, slouched down, his head resting on his fist, and I said, "What's going on? What's happened?" And he said, "Who the hell do you think you are?" I said, "What?" He said, "We have been waiting here for over an hour. Just who the hell do you think you are to keep these people waiting?" He pointed to the extras, the crew, everyone.

There was the most deathly hush. So I said, "I didn't know you were waiting for me. Why wasn't I called?" He said, "Don't give me that. Just how far do you think you can go? Just how much do you think you can get away with? What did you do when you came back from lunch?" I said, "Well, I had my lunch hour and I came back, I fixed my make-up, they ironed my dress and I've been waiting in the dressing room." He said, "I suppose you think that your make-up is more important than those people's make-up. I suppose you think your costume is more important than their costumes. Well, I have news for you. It isn't."

I said, "That wasn't what I meant. I've been waiting in there. No one called me." And he just stared at me. And the tears started coming down my face. Then I can't remember what happened. I guess he said something suitable like "Go to hell" or something unprintable. Then I got one of the assistant directors aside— there were five or six of them—and I said, "Was I supposed to be called?" He said, "Wait a minute, honey, I think

'Joe' was supposed to call you," and "Joe" thought "Sam" was supposed to call me and "Sam" thought "Tom" was supposed to call me and "Tom" thought "Henry" was supposed to call me.

The first assistant director went to Stevens and said, "Look, George, it turns out that no one delivered the message. The ball got fouled." Of course Stevens never said a word to me. Then I had to go out and act before all the extras that he'd done his tirade in front of. I was quivering—and in the scene I was supposed to cry. Now I've always wondered whether he did all that deliberately for the sake of the scene.

Years later he asked me to play Mary Magdalene, and I told him that after our last experience I was surprised that he asked me to be in a film. He appeared quite genuinely astounded. I said, "You mean you really don't remember?" He was quite hurt and he said, "I always thought we got along very well together."

The thing I really remember about *Giant*, the thing I'll never forget, was the night of Jimmy Dean's death. Jimmy had just finished his work in the film and was gone. The rest of us were sitting in the projection room, watching the rushes.

George shoots extensive footage on the smallest or the largest scenes—reels and reels and reels of film that he cuts down to maybe two angles. He's a brilliant editor. But he protects himself so thoroughly that you tend to become slightly cross-eyed, really satiated, by the time you've finished the scene. He will do what we call "clock"—shooting circularly from 12 to 6 and then moving closer for an inside clock, and then individual actors, and then shooting from up and then from down. By then, you really are kind of "puggled."

Anyway, those were the sorts of rushes we were watching. Suddenly the phone rang. I heard him say, "No, my God. When? Are you sure?" And he kind of grunted a couple of times and hung up the phone. He stopped the film and turned on the lights, stood up and said to the room, "I've just been given the news that Jimmy Dean has been killed."

There was an intake of breath. No one said anything. I couldn't believe it; none of us could. So several of us started calling newspapers, hospitals, police, the morgue. The news was not general at that time. After maybe two hours the word was confirmed.

Then everybody drifted out to their cars to go home. It was about nine o'clock at night; the studio was deserted. As I walked to my car, feeling numb, I saw a figure coming through the lights down one of the little side streets. It was George, getting into his Mercedes. We looked at each other, and I said, "I can't believe it, George, I can't believe it." He said, "I believe it. He had it coming to him. The way he drove, he had it coming."

A few months later there was another automobile tragedy. Michael's and my crow's-nest house had a murderous drive up to it—a real cork-twister. We gave a small dinner party. Rock Hudson was there, Monty Clift. Kevin McCarthy was there. It broke up around ten or ten-thirty. Very quiet. Monty left. He was tired, but had only taken about two drinks. Suddenly Kevin came lurching, white-faced, into the living room. He was saying something incoherent and finally one got the words. "My God, oh God, Monty's dead." We finally made out that Monty's car had crashed into a telephone pole about a block and a half down the hill.

We all ran down. My only thought

71

was to get into that car and Monty would be alive. The doors were jammed shut, but we could see that Monty's head looked like it had been mashed right into the steering wheel and the windshield was all broken, the dashboard was all smashed. He was bleeding from the head so much that it looked like his face had been halved.

Finally somebody got one of the doors open and we all kind of backed away from the car and then I crawled into the car and lifted him away from the steering wheel. I found that he was breathing and moaning. All my revulsion about blood absolutely left me. I held his head and he started coming to. You could hardly see his face. It was like pulp. He was suffering terribly from shock, but he was absolutely lucid. There was a tooth hanging on his lip by a few shreds of flesh, and he asked me to pull it off because it was cutting his tongue.

We had to wait forty-five minutes for the ambulance. It got lost. The ambulance came and we got him out of the car and, oh, God, it was horrible. He was squirting blood all over his face. He never once complained. I rode in the ambulance, and by the time we reached the hospital his head was so swollen that it was almost as wide as his shoulders. His eyes by then had disappeared. His cheeks were level with his nose. The whole thing was like a giant red soccer ball.

It wasn't till the doctors took him away that there was the shock of finding myself covered with somebody else's blood. The sick, sweet smell of it made me want to vomit. Later on I used to have nightmares about it and remember his face. It would come up like a balloon in front of me at night. His jaw had been broken in four places, his nose in two places, and he was badly cut around the eyes. And his upper lip—it was like a spoon had gouged a great big hunk out of his mouth and teeth. It all restored itself and he is still a beautiful man. He is beautiful inside. I think his looks are even more poignant now because they are not so perfect.

By this time, I am afraid that after five years my marriage with Michael Wilding had become the relationship for which we were much more suited— brother and sister. He's one of the nicest people I've ever known. But I'm afraid in those last years I gave him rather a rough time, sort of henpecked him, and probably wasn't mature enough for him. It wasn't that we had anything to fight over. We were just not happy, and I think it was showing in the two boys. Like little animals, they have antennae that can sense undercurrents.

Even during the divorce there was never any ugliness. It was friendly, if you can call a divorce that. He is married now to Margaret Leighton and they are so enchanting together. They're both so wildly witty in that awfully dry English way, and they're both so tall and thin. They're like two English matchsticks.

If I'm making everything sound too ho-hum, it was not. I wasn't desperate, but I was terribly upset. We had both failed—though I didn't blame him and he didn't blame me, thank God. And I knew that the children would always adore their father and that we would never have any competition for their affection, or anything like that. But I did not take it easily. I genuinely do not believe in divorce. I know that must sound pretty funny, coming from me.

CHAPTER FOUR

T HE FIRST TIME I ever saw Mike Todd was at the commissary at M-G-M. Somebody pointed out to me that that was the remarkable Mike Todd. And I thought, Oh, he's quite good-looking for a producer. He glanced at me a few times and I thought he had very pretty eyes Then, a couple of weeks later, Michael Wilding and I were invited to his house. I said, "What a lovely house." He answered, "Thank you—I designed it myself." I really believed it. I noticed that he had on a beautiful thin gold watch and matching flat band—I'd never seen one like it. He told me, "I designed it myself." I believed that. Any time Mike wanted to, he could always con me.

I had remembered seeing pictures of Mike in *Life* magazine surrounded by some *Peep Show* girls, while he sat in the middle with a huge cigar in his mouth. It had seemed extremely vulgar. But that day Mike was absolutely charming and attentive, and I thought, What a remarkable man he is—what energy and vitality. He doesn't seem vulgar at all. He seems quite a—well, not a gentleman— but a gentle man despite all of his shoutin' and bawlin'.

I saw him perhaps four times over a period of months—all at parties, once on his yacht. I remember once at his house there was one of those rubber divan things by the pool and we were sitting on it back to back, facing in opposite directions. Our backs were about three inches apart. I remember that gave me a weird but overpowering feeling. It was as though my spine were tingling. I finally got up and moved. Later I found out that the same kind of feeling was going through his back.

The first time, really, that we ever talked was when he proposed. The day after my separation from Michael Wilding was announced in the newspapers, I got a call from Mike Todd and he said, "I have to see you right away." He didn't ask me. He just told me. So I met

him at M-G-M and he was about half
an hour late. I'd gone into Benny Thau's
office and I was sitting there with my
feet on the table, drinking a Coca-
Cola.

Mike came over and picked me up by
the arm and without a word just dragged
me out of the office and took me down
the corridor, shoved me in an elevator
and went down another corridor—still
not speaking, just marching along breaking my arm—and went into a deserted office. He sort of plunked me on the couch,
and he pulled a chair around and started
in on a spiel that lasted about a half-
hour, saying that he loved me. And then
he said, "Don't horse around. You're going to marry me."

I looked at him the same way I
imagine a rabbit looks at a mongoose.
All kinds of things went through my
mind. I thought, Ah, well, he's stark,
raving mad. But I felt as though there
was an inevitable, overwhelming ava-
lanche kind of thing happening to me—
like sitting in quicksand and seeing it
coming up all over you and not being
able to move. But I didn't want to move.
I was so hypnotized I could easily have
said "Yes" right then. Then I thought,

Jeez, I've got to get away from this man, and I walked out in sort of a trance.

So I ran away from Mike—a couple of thousand miles away. I left immediately for Danville, Kentucky, to do *Raintree County*. I was looking forward to the film. Monty was well again and was in it with me. Mine was a strange part because the girl was really quite mad, which gave me a chance to climb up the walls and chew a lot of scenery. I thought, I'll really try to act and not just walk through it. So I enjoyed doing the film and I started to blossom a little and get confidence in myself.

Mike and I really got to know each other on the telephone, talking two or three hours a day—about what our tastes were, what we'd done during the day, what we wanted to do ten years from now, making jokes about everything. Every day he sent me huge bundles of flowers. I already knew about the Damon Runyan part of his personality. But his tenderness, his consideration, his enormous sensitivity, even vulnerability—they came completely unexpectedly to me. He was sensitive to poetry and music and art in a way that nobody would ever have suspected. I found he was very tuned in to the feelings of people around him. Mike was such a generously protective man.

There was never any second proposal after that first one. I had two weeks off from the shooting and Mike sent a special plane to bring me to New York. When the plane landed, he was out on the field waiting, and I ran down the steps into his arms and we kissed for the first time. There was no more discussion. That was it. We were getting married.

Shortly afterward came the premiere of *Around the World in Eighty Days,* and everybody knows what a fantastic success the film was. I've never seen anybody so excited in my life as Mike. We had a huge party afterward and announced our engagement to my family and his and I had a huge rock on my finger. It was all mad and marvelous.

Just before we were to get married, we had been to Nassau to see Lord Beaverbrook and were coming back on this huge, cumbersome sailing houseboat which tended to wallow rather like a whale. We were walking down this steep stairway and I was talking to Mike over my shoulder. The boat lurched and I went flying out into the air, feet out, and landed straight on my tail about six steps below. I was in terrible pain. When we landed in New York I said I had better see a chiropractor to pop the bone back in. Mike said, "You're not going to see any chiropractor. You're going to go to the Harkness Pavilion and see a proper bone man." "There's no need to," I said. "I'm sure there's nothing wrong with my back. I've had trouble with it all my life."

His chauffeur took me up to Presbyterian Hospital the next day. The doctors took X-rays and stuck pins in my back and tickled my feet and my legs with feathers. Then my doctor came back and said, "Well, I've just seen the X-rays and you're going into Room 703 right now." And I said, "No, I can't because Mike and I have a date to go to a party. We have to go." It was terribly posh and I had a brand-new dress and everything. "Honey," he said, "I don't know how you're walking around." Then Mike phoned and said, "Just keep your mouth shut and stay there."

In a few days I couldn't feel a feather at all. Even when they stuck the pins in my right leg and drew blood, I couldn't feel anything. I couldn't walk on it any more; the leg was paralyzed. Then it started to atrophy and began looking like a leg from Belsen.

I might have been panicky about never walking again if I hadn't had Mike to take care of me. And I had two beautiful children. I didn't care much whether I ever worked again or not, and you know, if you lose one leg, you've got another—and you've got your life.

Finally they operated. Three discs were absolutely gone. They cut away all the dead bone right down to the nerve center. They took bone from my hip, my pelvis and from a bone bank and made little matchsticks and formed clusters that finally calcified and became one long column, about six inches long.

Then the unbearably agonizing part began. I was absolutely paralyzed because the muscles had all been cut and my nervous center fiddled with. Every three hours, for two or three weeks, to keep the bone from sagging in any one position, they rotated me with sheets—a sheet pulling one way and a sheet pulling the other way rolls your body over. I felt rather like a pig on a spit.

If they give you enough of some drug to kill the pain, the side effects are dangerous. So when they rotate you, you pass out from the pain. It is so astronomical I can't remember it too well. But you hear this dreadful coward someplace in the hospital screaming and you think, "God, I wish they'd stop." Then you realize that it's yourself and then you burn up with pain and black out.

I was in a hospital bed for two months and had to learn to walk all over again. To move my legs was crunchville. My room really was the typical hospital room—a sort of pale vomit green. When Mike saw it, he went out and bought me a Renoir, a Pissarro and a Monet to hang there.

I got out looking terribly thin and feeling very svelte—and profoundly grateful to be walking—and terribly happy because we flew directly to Mexico and were married.

Mike Todd was a marvelous husband and a marvelous man. He spoke for himself and wherever he went, in seconds he'd be dominating and taking over. He had a joy, a relish about being alive, a vitality that was so contagious. He was a fabulous con artist—could con the gold out of your teeth—but was terribly, gregariously generous. His energy was unbounded—he slept only four hours a night. He was self-educated, not just out of books, but out of listening and curiosity. There wasn't a subject you could bring up that he wouldn't know something about. And if he didn't, he'd soon find out about it.

Some people kind of hated Mike. But they didn't know him. I think they were afraid of him, or jealous. If you didn't know the other Mike Todd, he could appear to be absolutely ruthless. He had a wild temper, but it was like a firecracker. It quickly erupted, was pretty colorful while it was there, but was quickly gone. And some didn't know how to cope with his authority, his sureness. The words "can't" and "impossible" were not in Mike's vocabulary at all.

Mike was strong, which was very good for me. I will get away with murder if I can. I used to try, out of my perversity, sometimes to drive Mike mad. I'd be late, deliberately just fiddle around and be late, and I loved it when he would lose his temper and dominate me. I would start to purr because he had won.

Mike made me feel complete. He made me feel confident that I could move on my own at a time when I was suffering from failure. He made me feel interesting, and not feel ashamed because I didn't know about things. He cut my inferiority complex in two and taught me to enjoy life.

Until then I had always gone to parties and really suffered—a silent, inarticulate lump, quaking with shyness. Actually, when I was married to Michael Wilding, it was Humphrey Bogart who had made me realize how bad I was. He really shouted and bawled at me. He said, "You just walk around in Michael's wake, you don't say anything, you just look at people with those eyes and don't contribute a thing. Sit down in that corner over there," he told me, "and make people come to you." So I tried it at a couple of parties and people did come over. And I started by talking about inane things—ordinary, everyday chit-chat—and it was like learning how to swim.

Today at parties, I'm some of the time more gregarious than Richard is—hopping and flitting, which I never could have done before. Richard you'll find usually in the center of the room with concentric rings of people around him while he's expounding. But among strangers I am still constipated with shyness—layers upon layers of it, a complete defensive shell. Don't show the chink. When I get like that, I seem very cool, very haughty. Faced with crowds, I want to run pell-mell through all those people with their little cameras and the flashbulbs they shoot off two feet from your eyes. But you make yourself walk and you find a point to focus your eyes on and keep going toward it.

Living with Mike Todd was like living with a circus. He used to call me almost every hour and maybe say, "I forgot to tell you last time that I love you. Good-bye." Then he might immediately send a wire saying, "How come I never hear from you?" Once, I'm told, he was in his car at a stop light. The phone in the car rang and he held it out the window and said to the man in the car next to him, "It's for you." And once he was talking on his car phone and wanted to get off, so he said, "Terribly sorry, but I'm wanted on the other phone."

He used to like me to come to the office, and he was fantastic to watch. He'd have ten different ideas going on at once. He'd have two telephones in his hands, a different conversation going on over each phone, plus a Dictaphone going. It was like an octopus with two hands and a brain at the end of each tentacle. But he always treated me as a partner and would ask me what I thought of something, and sometimes he'd even change his mind. He picked everyone's brains—taxicab drivers, the executives, the elevator boy.

One day he was trying to borrow some money for *Eighty Days* and got a moneybags on the phone. But he had arranged that Dick Hanley, who had become his secretary, would buzz him on another phone after a few minutes. Then, in a voice loud enough to be heard by Mr. Moneybags, he carried on a fake conversation, pretending to turn down somebody who wanted to invest in the film. By the time Mike got through, Moneybags thought Mike was doing him a favor by taking his money.

One of his favorite lines was "I not only lost a horse race, I lost a race track." Because he had. He had owned the Del Mar Race Track, bet it against a syndicate of men and lost.

One day we were sitting around talking about celebrating the first anniversary of *Eighty Days,* and Mike suddenly said, "We'll give it in Madison Square Garden." Then out poured all the plans as fast as he could think them up, and he went to work that moment on the phone. Well, the whole thing was an unmitigated disaster.

First, there was a circus parade up Eighth Avenue. Poor Sir Cedric Hardwicke rode on an elephant and almost fell off. There weren't enough policemen and they couldn't control the crowds and the parade literally couldn't get into the Garden on time where it was supposed to go around the ring. So it ended with a scramble of school bands, and elephants, and dogs and giraffes and horses and monkeys and cages full of birds, and thousands of people—all jumbled, sweaty, tugging, hauling.

There were thousands of gate crashers, and the waiters were hoarding the champagne and watering it down and selling it to people for ten dollars a bottle. I know; I got one of them. And my God, the sight of chic, lacquered women fighting with little kids to get a hamburger. Finally, Mike and I got home, and just the two of us got sloshed on real champagne. We stayed up till eight in the morning, hysterically laughing over all the things we'd seen go wrong.

Mike loved spoiling me, and I adored receiving presents—I mean, I love presents. There is certainly nothing blase about me in that area. He knew how much I loved paintings. He loved paintings, too, but instead of buying himself the paintings, he'd buy them for me. I think he liked to see me wear pretty jewelry. But sometimes he'd bring me a lipstick or something from the drugstore. It was just that when he went out, he usually would come back with something. It seemed to give him pleasure.

Our life together was not all lavish. We had some remarkably simple times —barbecues with the children, taking care of the house ourselves—no servants —going to bed early, reading, getting up early. We didn't go out every night— maybe out to dinner once or twice a week.

He was much more a feet-up-by-the-fireside kind of person than anyone knew. It was as though he wrote a script for how much outsiders were allowed to see, and the insiders were very few. The showman Mike Todd was a deliberately built public image, for you see, Mike, when he wasn't actually shooting a film, was selling the film. That involved showmanship; it involved being gregarious; it involved being Mike Todd, which was a full-time occupation.

We traveled all over the world together to promote *Around the World in Eighty Days*. Of course, we couldn't have gone more first class and we had a ball. We even had such fun fighting. We really were the most raucous fighters, no holds barred in public or otherwise. One time Mike got three transatlantic telephone calls at once, and we got to the London airport twenty minutes late and missed the plane for Nice. There was no other plane going. So you know, for once it was his fault and not mine. I was teasing him unmercifully and all these photographers and reporters were standing around. It was a kidding fight, but we were both using "Olde English" language and "Old Italian" gestures that are even better than language. Some photographer got a picture, and it was maybe Mike's favorite picture of us. I call it the only talking still picture in the world. I mean, there's no doubt about what we are saying to each other.

Finally, Mike chartered a huge airplane just for ourselves and we had all kinds of giggles going over. When we landed in Nice, there were about one hundred of the press waiting for us. They had heard we were getting a divorce.

On one trip I went to Russia. Mike was on some secret mission for the State Department that he never could tell me about. The Embassy was bugged, so he was always going for walks with the Ambassador. We were told that our hotel room was bugged, so we'd say loudly, "I wish we had tickets to the Bolshoi two days from now. I think they're doing *Swan Lake*." "Yes, Mike, did you ask at Intourist?" "Yes, but they said they didn't have any. Isn't that a shame?" And the next day you'd have two tickets.

What impressed me most, I think, on the trip to Russia was the circus. It was the epitome of skill and the epitome of naivete. They had a hippopotamus to whom the man would say, "Roll over," and it would roll over. Then the hippopotamus would open its mouth with teeth the size of my thighs, and the man would put his whole body inside its mouth and it would hobble around on a couple of legs. But after that extraordinary, unique act, a little lady in a blue taffeta dress came out and played the accordion—you know, little bows in the hair, puff sleeves, and lace gloves. It was so endearing because it was so incongruous.

But the thing that was the most fascinating was the audience. There were men in those powerful-looking uniforms that had big shoulder padding and epaulets. They had leather boots that came up to the knees and medals all over, and everything a somber, very serious color. Maybe one-third of the audience would be these great, thick, burly soldiers and officers. The rest of the audience were little old men and women with grandchildren.

And practically every face in the audience, at one time or another, would cry from their laughter. You never see that in the Western world—people laughing so ingenuously, so totally. I was absolutely captivated, because they had the kind of naivete that we've lost. We're ashamed to laugh that thoroughly. And I felt so warm toward them. I thought, These people here can't be our enemies. It's the people running the governments we should be afraid of.

One of my sharpest memories is the sight in the streets of Moscow—every morning, every afternoon, at night—of bundled-up, ruddy-faced women in their thirties, forties, fifties, sixties and seventies, standing in long lines shoveling away the snow from the entrances of the hotels and public buildings. And in the street, walking, the people are like subways, subway trains of human beings on the snow—a never-ending, never-ceasing line of traffic like a mobile train moving in and out of the buildings on the snow. And it was all kind of gray, all the same color.

This was the first place I'd ever been that I could sit and observe people. Usually, I am watched. I can't watch in return, because then it becomes a challenge.

This was also the first time in my adult life I'd been completely anonymous— though I guess we weren't exactly anonymous. First of all, I wore lipstick and my hair had just been done in Paris and I wore mascara. It was twenty below zero and I had marvelous fur-lined high red leather boots, a full mink coat, and a diamond ring like a skating rink on my finger. So they knew we were slightly different.

People would come over and they'd smile and touch my fur and they'd say to the interpreter, "What is she, a ballerina?" They never said "actress." The epitome of glamour in Russia, I guess, is a ballerina. But there was a real *gemütlich* feeling. There was no jealousy or envy involved, just gentleness and a great unspoken rapport. And it wasn't because they admired us or because we were famous.

In the Western world, when you're recognized, there's a sort of derisive, condescending look that includes the head, the toe and back up again—like, "Who do you think you are?" And indeed sometimes one wonders.

I know I'm lucky. I know when I wear a lovely Dior gown and jewels and a nice hair style that I'm bloody lucky. But the kind of looks that you get from some people are so filled with—I don't know exactly what the word is. It's a kind of envy, jealousy, dislike, because you have the trappings and they don't. You very rarely get the kind of genuine, unselfish thing that I experienced in Russia—a sort of "Isn't that lovely?" or "Isn't that a beautiful coat?" In the Western world, sometimes, you find that people don't *like* you to have superficial material things, even though we all have the same chance of getting them. People don't have that kind of chance in Russia, but *we* do.

Look at Mike Todd. Mike had no education. His father was an out-of-work rabbi. At the age of seven he would go into a cafeteria, and he was so tiny and undernourished he'd sneak up to a table and drink out of a bottle of catsup and the pitcher of milk and eat the sugar on the table. When he was nineteen, he was a millionaire in the construction business. He had a knack, of course, for earning money. But it went way beyond that, because he was a very learned, cultured man and that was all his own doing.

Richard Burton is a miner's son from a tiny village in Wales. Richard got his education through the scholarships he won by intuition and drive and ambition and lust for learning and a great love of words. Without those he would be down in the mines. He never would have made it. But both men did make it, didn't they? So anyone can.

I once told Mike that I hoped we'd have a girl because the world couldn't take two Mike Todds. And little did I know I would end up with a female Mike Todd. When I was pregnant with Liza, it was only a few months after my back operation and the doctors thought the pressure from the embryo would push the newly formed bone right out and cripple me. They had a meeting and decided the baby should be aborted. I said, "Not on your nelly." And they explained why it must happen. And I explained why it was not going to happen.

So they fixed up my back brace with elastic gussets over my stomach to make room for Liza. I almost lost her three times. One time, crossing the Atlantic, I started having labor pains. I'd had two Caesareans and a normal childbirth was impossible. The doctor on that boat, he certainly didn't know how to perform a Caesarean. I got the feeling he thought babies came out of your nose.

I started having labor pains every twenty minutes, fifteen minutes, ten minutes—down to five minutes, with contractions of the stomach and the whole thing. Mike was going absolutely mad, calling my New York gynecologist every half-hour on the phone. Finally, they decided just to knock me out to try and stop the spasms, and that worked. When I got to New York, I went straight to the hospital. I was in an oxygen tent for two weeks.

Eventually, my back brace pushed the baby way up under my ribs and moved my heart over a couple of inches, which made me faint all the time. And I had a tremendously high pulse. So the doctors finally said, "We'll have to take the baby." I begged them to wait—a week, a day, anything. I told them, "She's not cooked yet."

They took the baby that afternoon. And she was stillborn. Liza didn't breathe for fourteen and a half minutes. They told Mike, "Your wife, we think, will be all right, but the baby's dead." They had a resuscitationist in the delivery room who worked on the baby for fourteen and a half minutes. Then Liza took a breath. She was in the hospital in an oxygen tent for almost two months.

Mike went to see her. She weighed four pounds. Liza made a little convulsive gesture with one arm. No power on earth could ever have convinced Mike that Liza wasn't waving to him. He bought her a little gold hairbrush from Tiffany's. He had had engraved on it: "Dear Liza, I wanted to buy you platinum, but Mommy says I shouldn't spoil you."

Mike and I had been married thirteen months when he was chosen Showman of the Year and was to be guest of honor at a dinner in New York on Saturday, March 22, 1958. It was all arranged that he and I would fly east for it. I had even arranged for time off from *Cat on a Hot Tin Roof,* which I had begun. But on Wednesday of the week before, I was sent home from the studio with a terrible bronchitis condition. My temperature kept going higher and higher, and all my life I've suffered from respiratory complications. I begged Mike to let me go along anyway. We had never been apart overnight before. He *had* to go. They had sold so many tickets, and Mike was too professional to let them down. After talking to our doctor, Rex Kennamer, he decided it was too dangerous for me. And it *was* only for two days.

Mike had to leave on Friday night. The weather was absolutely miserable all day, pouring rain. In the afternoon Mike, with his tremendous energy, played with Christopher and Michael, and they all got into the big sunken bathtub we had and were ducking each other, splashing water, squirting each other with water pistols, just having a marvelous time horsing around. From where I lay on my bed with my 102 temperature, I could see them reflected in my dressing table mirrors. They were so happy—I was so happy watching them. Then it was time for him to leave—he'd delayed to the absolute last minute.

Mike kissed me good-bye and we hugged each other. He went down the stairs. The next thing I knew he was back up the stairs again and he was holding me again and we kissed good-bye again. There was this terrible feeling of premonition that we both had. And he said, "I'm too happy. I'm so afraid something's going to happen. I'm too happy." And I guess we both cried. Then he left again. Suddenly, in a matter of seconds, kind of shamefacedly, almost apologetically, he was back again. And each of the five or six times we said good-bye, I would close my eyes.

And you know, it was *me* he was wor-

ried about. I don't think he considered
something happening to him. He absolutely believed in our little toy airplane.
He called it the "Liz" and never worried
about flying.

After Mike had left—without a coat
—I couldn't sleep. I was terribly worried
and the night was really Macbethian—
the lightning and thunder and the rain.
Bea, the children's nurse, came up about
five in the morning to put rubbing al-
cohol on my back, because I was boiling
hot.

I had this feeling. I tried to rationalize
it. I thought, It's because I don't feel
well. It's because we've never been really
separated. It's because it's such a fierce
night and I'm just being superstitious.
And, of course, the way he said good-bye
to me, that upset me terribly.

Mike had promised he would call me
when they landed in Albuquerque to re-
fuel, which would have been about six in
the morning my time. So I waited by the
phone from six o'clock on. When the call
didn't come through, I thought, Well, he
probably thinks I'm asleep. Bea had left
by then. The kids were still asleep. Six-
thirty, nothing. Seven o'clock, nothing. I
began to panic, but then I thought, No,

it must be because he thinks I'm asleep. And I waited and waited.

About eight-thirty, the door opened and Rex Kennamer was in the doorway with Dick Hanley. I thought Rex had just come by to see how I was, and I guess I smiled and said, "Hi, Rex, how are you?" His face seemed strange and I looked at Dick and they were both just looking at me and I shot up in bed and screamed "No!" And they said "Yes." It was like you read or see in movies—where people can't say the word "dead." Then all I could do was scream "No" and I ran downstairs and all through the house and out into the street with my nightgown on. Rex caught me and knocked me out with a drug.

I flew to the funeral in Chicago. They tried to keep me from doing that, but I knew that I could never forgive myself if I didn't go. Rex went with me and kept me under sedation during the funeral—thank God, because it was total horror. I only remember it in nightmarish vignettes. Very sweetly, Howard Hughes had given me a big TWA plane with the crew, so I didn't have to go on a regular airline and have people gawk. But as we drove out to the cemetery—I had on a black hat with a small black veil—not a "widow's weed" hat at all, but a hat Mike had given me—I remember going past a factory and hearing a couple of young girls yell out, "Oh, dig that crazy widow's veil."

There were, the police estimated, over ten thousand people *in* the cemetery. Now this was in March—a howling Chicago March. And they were sitting on tombstones with blankets spread out. I remember seeing bags of potato chips in the wind. And empty Coca-Cola bottles. And children crawling over tombstones. And as the car pulled up, they all broke away from their picnic lunches, came screaming like black-gray birds to the car—all squawking and screaming and yelling in our ears as if it were some sort of premiere.

Fortunately, there was a tent over the actual grave. But all during the ceremony the people outside were yelling, "Liz, Liz. Come on out, Liz. Let's have a look." After the coffin was lowered into the ground, I asked everybody to leave. I knelt and said a prayer and went out by myself. And then the crowd broke loose —the police couldn't hold them back— and rushed at me. My brother Howard was holding me and they started tearing the veil from my hat for souvenirs. Finally, Howard got me to the car, but by then we'd lost the driver. They swarmed like insects all over the car so you couldn't see out the windows. For ten minutes the driver couldn't get to the car. The car was rocking. Then I started screaming.

People just don't behave like that. But they do.

A week after Mike's death—I had been really out of my senses and in bed and under sedation—I got up and went downstairs. We had this big, dark, Mediterranean-type house and we hardly ever used the living room, which was arched and singularly gloomy. As I came down the circular staircase on terribly wobbly legs, I heard a tiny, high, little voice singing in the kind of monotone chant you hear in church, "Mike is dead! Mike is dead! Mike is dead!" It was little Michael. He was standing by a window. I could see his silhouette and I could see his face was all wet.

The shirt Mike had been wearing before he left, the pajamas he'd had on— I kept them under the pillow. There was a little smell of Mike left. I wouldn't let them change the sheets for weeks. I kept everything just the same in our closets. Then suddenly I couldn't bear to look at his things. So I had them packed away. You have to watch not to build a shrine.

CHAPTER FIVE

I THINK I WAS SLIGHTLY around the bend after Mike's funeral. I couldn't read; I couldn't watch television; I couldn't do anything. I couldn't eat. I threw up a lot, but I was not hysterical. After a few days I went down to stay with my brother and his wife. We really love each other. Sometimes they'd let me have their bed and sometimes I'd sleep in a sleeping bag. I'd go to the beach with their kids and I started going for walks. I was getting better.

I had been working on *Cat on a Hot Tin Roof* for two weeks when Mike died, and having that to finish saved me in a way. I couldn't tolerate what I was, and it gave me somebody else to become. When I was Maggie was the only time I could function. The rest of the time I was a robot. When they said "Cut," I would go back to my dressing room, and I don't remember much what I did. I would just more or less stare vacantly. I still couldn't eat—except for popcorn, for some peculiar reason.

There was one scene in the film where I had to eat, and usually food on a movie set is all covered with fly spray and left there all day under the lights. But Burl Ives kept making sure the prop boys put newly baked ham on my plate and corn bread, and I ate for the first time. They kept shooting the scene over and over again, and each time I ate and ate and ate.

But it was a cruel film to be making at that time—all about death. There was one line Judith Anderson had to say to me: "I guess things never turn out the way you dream they are going to turn out." Mike and I had planned our lives up to age one hundred. The one thing neither of us planned on was death. Mike didn't even have any life insurance.

It took me a long time to accept the fact that Mike was dead. I was racked with the wish that I had been in that plane, and maybe I had a sense of guilt that I wasn't. A dream that came over and over was the crash itself. In the dream I was in the plane and I would go through the panic of the falling plane and the fire and I could see the whole thing happening. It was like a falling dream; you wake just before you hit the bottom. And sometimes I evidently woke up screaming because I would disturb other people in the house. And for years, until I started *Cleopatra,* until I met Richard, I would dream at night that Mike was still alive and he would come to me. And I would dream that what I had been going through in the daytime was only a nightmare that I would wake from.

I even used to wear Mike's wedding ring. It was curious, because the plane was so completely burned out, and gold melts easily—but the only thing they found in the plane was the ring I put on his finger during the ceremony. It was twisted and burned and charred, but I never took it off until three years ago. If I couldn't wear it in a film, I'd pin it to my underclothing. It was like I was still married to Mike. I was married to a ghost and the ghost was more alive to me than any human being.

To get away, I decided to make a trip to Europe. En route I stopped in New

York for a visit. Eddie Fisher was there —Eddie who had been one of Mike's best friends, and had idolized Mike to the point of trying to make himself over in his image. I knew Eddie was not very happy. I knew he loved to talk about Mike almost as much as I did. So we went out in public together several times —and all hell broke loose. The press and the public—the whole world—was convinced that I was breaking up a perfectly happy marriage. Instead of keeping on my way and going to Europe as I intended, I thought, My God, poor Eddie. And we went back to Hollywood.

There were times there with Eddie when I would go into a restaurant or somewhere and people that I knew would suddenly be deep in conversation as I went by the table. Or if I'd say hello, there would be a brief nod of the head. So then I really cut myself off from everybody.

One time I telephoned someone and asked if I could drive out to his house. It was near the beach, and I felt absolutely trapped. He said something like "Oh, I'm terribly sorry, darling, we're going out to the beach with the children, but we'll be back around seven. I'll call you later." Well, I didn't hear from him or his wife for seven months.

Now, in my steady, gnawing grief for Mike, I felt a desperate need for a formalized religion. I had discovered that I had no way of expressing myself in prayer other than an almost wordless howl to God—"Oh, God, oh God, oh God." I wanted something more channeled, more profound, more satisfying.

I had been brought up a Christian Scientist, and I think that has many merits. But when I was young, I began asking questions which didn't seem to have any answers, so most of my adult life I was just nothing. During the war as a kid I had Walter Mitty dreams about being Jewish and wishing I was. I don't know why I thought that being Jewish and living in California I could help Jewish children in Germany. But later I did read up on Judaism, and after Mike and I were married, I had told him that I wanted to be a Jewess. He said, "Be slow, be deliberate, be careful. Don't do it on account of me. In ten years, then do it."

But when he died, I really needed it. I studied for about nine months, went to the temple regularly and converted. I am absolutely Jewish now in my beliefs and feelings, although I am not very good about going to synagogue. My Jewish name is Elisheba Rachel. I wanted to use Ruth instead of Rachel, but it had too many memories. Mike and I had a continuing joke in which I said, "Whither thou goest, I will go too, Buster!"

I picked the Reform philosophy because it has a gentleness, an understanding, a largeness that makes me feel quiet and calm and gentle inside. It's very live-and-let-live, and remarkably lacking in hypocrisy. I really don't know about the Orthodox, and I don't think I'd like it because it's too inundated with ceremony. Everything is in Hebrew, and I like to hear what's going on. That's why I don't feel too awfully guilty about not going very often to the synagogue. I pray in the bath, in closets, when I'm putting my shoes on. I'm one of those people who think you can be close to God anywhere, not just in a place designated for worship and built with millions of pesos, while maybe people are starving outside.

Sometimes I think that I'd rather give the money to the people, so they won't have rickets or suffer from malnutrition. But, of course, it's a wonderful thing to have a gorgeous place to worship. It's like, in a minor way, the English with their royalty and their tradition. It's like the Spanish with their bullfighting, like the Russians with their ballerinas. Maybe real gold and real gems inside a church really lift people into another world. And probably all that gold and all those gems wouldn't feed them anyway. But I still don't understand it.

The most appalling thing that happens to me as a Jewess is when people make an exception for me. On a trip to Washington, Mike had to see a Senator from the gentle South. The word "Jew" entered the conversation and Mike, with all his openness, said, "Well, you know, Senator, you're talking to a Jew." The Senator said, "Really, how are you Jewish?" And Mike said, "Just on my mother's and father's side." The Senator said, "Well, you're what I'd consider a White Jew." Mike evidently picked up the desk and practically wrapped it around the guy's neck. As Mike used to say, he hadn't been so mad since he was Jewish.

On top of having lost Mike I almost lost Liza, too. She had double pneumonia when she was eighteen months old and such a tiny thing. She was completely unconscious and sort of blue-gray. They punctured her lumbars and had great big pipes going into her little chest. There were great big needles going into her veins, and her little arms were strapped onto boards taped to the bed. They don't actually say to you, "She's not going to live." They say, "Her chances are very slim." And you pin them down. "What are the odds? Would you put it in numbers so I can understand?" "Well, her chances of survival are ten percent"— which is really about nothing.

So for three days there was almost no hope at all. Then her color began coming back. "She has a fifty-fifty chance," they said. It was like being given life. If she had died, that really would have been the end. I don't think I could have borne that.

Through all those months of grief for Mike, I felt that I had loved and that there would never be anything like that again in my life. Eddie, who loved Mike, too, was the one man who could understand that my heart would always belong to the memory of Mike. And Eddie, somehow, made Mike seem more alive.

At the same time I felt cold and

trapped by circumstances and without any of my own resources to find a way out. Maybe with Eddie I was trying to see if I was alive or dead. Also, for some idiotic reason, I thought that Eddie needed me, and I should make *somebody* happy. Anyway, we got married.

It was clearly a mistake. We both, I think, tried very hard, but the marriage was untenable—for both of us. To describe the indignities we inflicted on each other—and so many others—would be too private to go into. It was clearly a mistake, and also I don't want to hurt Eddie. I have done too much of that already.

My first film after I got married was *Suddenly Last Summer*. Most of the advisers that one has in show business said, "You mustn't do it; it won't make a penny at the box office; it's too raw." My feeling was that my first independent venture, free of M-G-M, should be one that I wanted to do artistically. I didn't really care whether it devaluated me. I wanted to do that part; I enjoyed acting it; and curiously enough, it did not lay a bomb.

One day in London where we were doing the interior scenes of *Suddenly*

Last Summer the phone rang and Eddie answered. It was Walter Wanger saying he wanted me to play *Cleopatra*. I thought the idea was ridiculous and said to Eddie, "Tell him it will cost him a million dollars"—you know, ha, ha. Walter said okay.

M-G-M knew about it. At that time I was free of M-G-M, but they had the right to pre-empt my services at any time for one more film—and they decided to do this to prevent me from doing *Cleopatra*. Somebody figured that if I ever got a big chunk of money under my belt, I'd retire and they'd never get their film. So I had to do *Butterfield 8*.

I was appalled, not just over losing the money but because of the way the whole situation had come about. I had had three years more to go on my contract when M-G-M wanted me to do *Cat on a Hot Tin Roof*. Mike went in and said, "This is going to be her last film for M-G-M or she will not do the film." And they said, "You know we'll put her on suspension," and he said, "Fine. Nothing would make me happier. She wants to retire anyway." They said, "Oh, you mean and not do anything else?" And he said, "Oh, that's exactly what I mean."

M-G-M decided they'd rather have *Cat* than nothing, so they said okay, and they shook hands.

Not long after Mike was dead, M-G-M with their usual gallantry announced that it had been a verbal deal with Mike, but since he no longer existed, the deal no longer existed, and I had a three-year contract with them again. Now I was in no coherent state to be making business deals and fighting the studio. I was so sickened by their tactics that I told them I guessed I'd just retire then. So they said, "You finish *Cat on a Hot Tin Roof* and give us one film after that, and we'll let you off." The only reason I agreed was that I was so dead and lost that I thought the only way to keep my sanity was to do something, a job, and the only job I knew was acting. Also, the film was almost an obligation to Mike. He had such a sense of professionalism, and I had to make Mike proud of me. I had to stay alive, and the only reason was for Mike—until I met Richard.

Butterfield 8 was bringing me in maybe $125,000, which of course is a lot of money, but it was not a script of my choice, and I had been *ordered* to do it, even though I thought it was dreadful. After shooting for two weeks, the whole motion picture industry was closed down by strikes for about two months. So I got four friends of mine who were top playwrights and screenwriters, names to conjure with, and I gave them the script, and said, "Look, please help me. I can't say these lines." They couldn't do it legally because they were on strike, so I said, "If you'd just give me some ideas for dialogue, I'll say they're mine." So I had four of the top writers in the industry give me some changes, many of them key lines. I went with them to the producer and the director. The producer said, "Look, honey, we can't have these amateurish lines in the film, so be a good girl and just relax and don't meddle in it." Like I was a little girl dreaming them up in the nighttime.

I got the Academy Award for *Butterfield 8*. The reason was, I am afraid, that I had come within a breath of dying of pneumonia only a few months before. I was filled with profound gratitude at being considered by the industry an actress and not a movie star. My eyes were wet and my throat awfully tight. But I knew my performance had not deserved it, that it was a sympathy award. And it was all very dramatic because my leg was still hugely bandaged. Infection set in where they had been feeding me intravenously, and I'd almost lost the leg.

When I became sick with pneumonia, I think it was my subconscious which let me become so seriously ill. I just let the disease take me. I had been hoping to be happy, pretending to be happy. But there was something deeply desperate inside me and I was consumed by self-pity. I had stopped thinking, I had stopped reading, I had stopped discussing anything—just numbly agreed with everything Eddie said. I became just sort of stupid. And my despair became so black that I just couldn't face waking up any more, couldn't face another divorce. My dream world which was Mike was much more satisfactory and much more real. As I've said, I was not a very healthy girl. Poor Eddie. What hell all that must have been for him.

I really believe that whole lives can have turning points. Mine came with that pneumonia. I was at a hotel because I have a terrible fear of hospitals—that awful, antiseptic smell, that sort of soft, squishy sound of nurses' footsteps. The nurse discovered that I was blue, that I had stopped breathing and my nails were starting to turn black. I was suffocating, and she picked up the phone and called for a doctor. Near my room there was a party being given for a young medical student who was getting married. The hotel operator figured that there would be doctors there, and one of the greatest anesthesiologists and resuscitationists *was* there. This man in his dickey bow and tails came flying down the corridor. He picked me up by the heels and tried to make me lose some of the congestion in my chest by making me sick. And nothing happened. And then he stuck his fist down my throat to make me gag. Nothing happened. Then he started hitting me on the chest to break up the congestion. Nothing happened. Then he started gouging at my eyes, because even in the deepest coma you evidently react to pain. So he gouged away like mad and I opened my eyes—now mind you, when I went to bed I'd just had a nice dinner with Yul Brynner. In my next moment of consciousness I decided somebody was taking advantage of me. I took a breath which kept me alive

118

and said, "Why don't you bug off," and then went crash out again for six days.

They got me to the hospital, slit open my throat and stuck a pump down to take this stuff out of my lungs—which if you molded it into a ball and threw it on the floor would bounce. I did come to on the operating table. Everybody had green caps, green masks, green outfits—and this huge, blazing light was over my head. I tried to say the usual bromide, "Where am I?" But the breath just blew out through the gash in my throat—a big wound mouth. I couldn't even whisper. Now you can't imagine how terrifying that is. That's when I thought maybe I was dead. Then I became aware of this terrible contraption and that I couldn't move. My whole body was paralyzed. But I guess my eyelids were moving, my mouth was trying to move. I don't know how long nobody noticed—I screamed inside—like one of those awful horror stories you read of somebody waking up in a coffin.

Finally, one of the nurses saw that my eyes were open and there must have been a look of such terror in my eyes, because she bent over and told me that I was in the London Clinic and that I was going to be all right. And I knew I was going to die. I gestured that I wanted to write something, because the feeling of being unable to communicate was more frightening than anything. And I wrote, "Am I still dying?" The writing looked like that of a 190-year-old creature—it took up a whole page. Then I went into another coma.

They had a terrible time taking that awful stuff out of my lungs. Four times after the initial time, I stopped breathing. Once I started to go when I was awake. I tried to draw a breath and nothing happened. I could feel the oxygen leaving my whole system. Instead of blood it was like boiling water flowing through my whole body, and it was like tons on my chest and the terrible thing of pulling, sucking, and not being able to get any breath, and finally getting dizzy. There was a scream in my head and the pain as the oxygen started to leave my brain—scorching pain—and then the noise. And I screamed with prayers. I wanted to live, I prayed to God to live. All I had time for was a silent scream—"Oh God, oh God."

After one of those times that I didn't know about, I woke up feeling so tranquil. It sounds crazy. I remember dreaming that I had talked to Mike. Now that sounds, you know, just kind of too, too weird. But when I woke up, I was so filled with awe that I told a couple of doctors. I know they thought I was around the bend, but I wasn't afraid any more.

When I came to that last time, it was like being given sight, hearing, touch, sense of color. Like I was, I don't know, twenty-nine years old, but had just come out of my own womb. I knew that I wanted more in my life than what I had.

CHAPTER SIX

WHEN I GOT pneumonia, I was working in London on Walter Wanger's production of *Cleopatra*. The part was still uncast when I finished *Butterfield 8*. By the time I had recovered enough to work again, the original *Cleopatra* company had been completely dissolved, the script rewritten, Joe Mankiewicz made director—and prime writer—the site moved to Rome, and the whole project inflated to the most Gargantuan scale. Even my dressing room was five times normal. I was involved with *Cleopatra* for five years on and off, and surely that film must be the most bizarre piece of entertainment ever to be perpetrated—the circumstances, the people involved, the money spent.

Everything was such a nightmare that it is difficult even to know where to start.

123

It had some curious effect on just about every person who worked on it. The whole thing was sick: people spying, spying on each other, unseen factions. "Spectre" back home—you know, Twentieth Century-Fox—was trying to oust Spyros Skouras, so there was a whole battery of pressures that had absolutely nothing to do with making *Cleopatra*. On all fronts, the politics that were going on, the frame-up jobs, the blackmail, the lying; it was incredible. Really, it was James Bondesque-ish.

The first day I saw Richard Burton on the *Cleopatra* set, there was a lot of hemming and hawing, and he said hello to Joe Mankiewicz and everyone. And then he sort of sidled over to me and said, "Has anybody ever told you that you're a very pretty girl?" And I said to myself, *Oy gevaldt,* here's the great lover, the great wit, the great intellectual of Wales, and he comes out with a line like that. I couldn't believe it. I couldn't wait to go back to the dressing room where all the girls were and tell them.

The way I began falling in love with Richard was very funny, really. He was kind of a legend in the theater and in films. He is a pro to the extent—well, it kind of boggles your imagination. For instance, I know of no other film actor who knows the whole script, everybody's lines, the day before he starts working. Now, that's a sweet, enchanting mania. I mean, he really is a banshee, but completely captivating.

I had met Richard before at Stewart Granger's house. My first impression was that he was rather full of himself. I seemed to remember that he never stopped talking and I had given him the cold fish eye. So I figured that now Richard would come along, the Old Vic actor, and sort of throw the cues to Rex if he dried up, and before I even opened my mouth he'd probably be throwing me my cues. And I was really very resentful, probably because I envied his Shakespearean background, and the fact that he was not a movie star but a genuine actor.

Well, the first day we were to work together I've never seen a gentleman so hung over in my whole life. He was kind of quivering from head to foot and there were grog blossoms—you know, from booze—all over his face. He ordered a cup of coffee to sort of still his trembling fits and I had to help it to his mouth,

125

and that just endeared him so to me. I thought, Well, he really is human. He was so vulnerable and sweet and shaky and terribly giggly that with my heart I *"cwtched"* him—that's Welsh for "hug."

Then when it was time to do some work, he blew a line. If it had been a planned strategic campaign, Caesar couldn't have planned it better. My heart just went out to him.

Another time, Eddie and I went out to dinner with Richard and Sybil and Roddy McDowall. Eddie and I had gone out maybe four times during six or seven months. Especially after work, I love to change clothes, take a bath and go out. It's like a snake shedding a dry skin— and you do feel dry and tight when you come home from the studio. With Eddie, usually we'd eat dinner in our pajamas. Eddie didn't drink then and he didn't like me to have more than one glass of wine.

That evening Richard was sitting across the table from me and it was about nine-thirty and Eddie kept saying, "Well, now, I better take you home; you have to get to bed early." And I kept saying, "Please let's stay a little longer." Richard evidently saw the expression on my face. I was keyed up and having a marvelous time and I really didn't want to go. So Richard, talking very busily to distract Eddie, kept taking my empty glass and exchanging it with his full one. I thought, I absolutely adore this man.

As we got to know each other better, Richard very slowly, very carefully, very gently pointed out to me that there were things that were a part of me that I hadn't even noticed—like every single photograph in the house was of Mike. The fact that I wore only Mike's wedding ring. I would leave my other wedding ring behind sometimes. I would talk only about Mike. I had been living four years in the past—not further behind and not further forward. And I began to realize from his very gentle points that it was selfish. He was like Prince Charming kissing the sleeping princess.

By myself, one by one I packed away all the relics. But the more layers of insulation I peeled off, the more dreadful my everyday life became. Now Eddie and I didn't even have Mike in common. But I *had* to build myself back up into a human being. I started to take more care of myself. I started to look ahead and live in the present. I started to live for my children again.

There was never any point at which Richard and I began. We just loved each other, and there was no discussion of it. I mean it was there—a fact of our lives. We didn't want it to happen because of Sybil and their children. She and I weren't close friends or anything, but I admired Sybil tremendously and loved being around her. And Richard and I really fought and hurt each other terribly to keep it from happening. My God, we told each other to leave a hundred times. It was really more off than on.

According to the code of ethics today, I was, I suppose, behaving wrongly because I broke the conventions. But I didn't feel immoral then, though I knew what I was doing, loving Richard, was wrong. I never felt dirty, because it never was dirty. I felt terrible heartache because so many innocent people were involved. But I couldn't help loving Richard. I don't think that was without honor. I don't think that was dishonest. It was a fact I could not evade.

There was terrible pain. Whether Richard existed or not, Eddie and I were trying to hold on. But one of the things he did—I was in Rome, he was in New York—the telephone rang and it was

Eddie calling me. He told me that he'd called a press conference. He said he wanted me to tell them that there was no foundation for the stories coming out of Rome. And I said, "Well, Eddie, I can't do that because there is some truth in the story. I just can't do that." And he said, "Wait a minute, what do you mean you won't do that?" And I said, "I can't say that because it's not true. There is a foundation to the story." And he said, "Thanks a lot!" And then he hung up. Eddie and I never did live together again.

And what ballooned the unbelievably Wagnerian, insane quality of everything was the insanity going on at the *Cleopatra* set every day. They would actually misplace fifteen hundred spears. And when the expenses began mounting astronomically, suddenly the great way to save money was: "We've got to cut down on the number of paper cups used."

One day Rex Harrison came out from his house on the Via Antiqua and there was his chauffeur with a Mercedes-Benz. So Rex said, "Where's my Cadillac?" The chauffeur said, "They think it's too expensive." So Rex rode in this car, stalked onto the set and said, "Where's

129

the money man?"—who soon appeared. "Where is my car?" demanded Rex in his best Henry Higgins voice. The money man said, "Ah, ah, well, we, ah, felt that perhaps you wouldn't mind a Mercedes because it's a little cheaper." And Rex went stark, staring mad and said, "I want my Cadillac and I want it now. And I do not appear on the set until my Cadillac is back. And what's more, I understand that Elizabeth Taylor's chauffeur is being paid far more than my chauffeur. I insist that my chauffeur get the same pay as Elizabeth Taylor's chauffeur. Why the hell should Elizabeth Taylor's chauffeur get more than my chauffeur just because she has a bigger chest!"

Of course, the Cadillac was from a car-hire firm, and since it wasn't in use by Mr. Harrison that day, it had taken some American couple to Pompeii—so Mr. Harrison didn't work one day. So their little economy probably cost them plenty that day. And at that stage in the film, I think any of us would have done just what Rex did.

One day this kind of thing happened. Joe Mankiewicz was attempting the enormous task of directing all day and then at night being a writer to combat Shaw and Shakespeare. Notice the title of the film: "Mankiewicz's *Cleopatra*," so people wouldn't get it screwed up with Shakespeare's or Shaw's *Cleopatra*.

He wrote a scene in which I hit Richard across the face a couple of times, and then when he bashed me across the face, I had to literally fly back through the air eight or nine feet and land—with my bad back, mind you—precisely on a marked spot. Then Richard, with me lying on the floor, had to move up about five short steps and, like a machine gun, deliver a tirade about three pages long. Richard was very worried about having to hit me without hurting me, but at the same time making it look like real hell. Very dicey bit, that.

It took two or three hours to get everything set up. I went up to Richard and bashed him across the face; we had the initial dialogue, and bash, down I went right on the mark, and the cameramen —marvelous technicians—moved perfectly with Richard as he did his enormous speech. It was all dead on, and when he finished, the entire place, hundreds of technicians, actors standing around, all applauded. So Mankiewicz

131

says, "Okay, let's do it again." "Why?" "For protection."

So we do it again, dead on. "Let's leave it till tomorrow," he says. The following morning, we do it again. Another two, three times. Nothing wrong. Nobody ever said to either of us that anything was wrong. When we finished, I was shaking.

Another part of the nightmare was a woman in the company who kept calling up a hairdresser's husband and saying, "I'm a friend of yours. Your wife is fooling around with somebody." Then she would hang up. Not only did this woman call the husband up when he was in Rome, but when—working on a film—he was sent to Portugal, she found him there and called him. "You better come back," she said. "Your wife is messing around with someone."

One of the wardrobe women, who was single, was having an amour with an Italian man on the film who was definitely married. This unknown spy found out the Italian man's home number, kept calling up the wife and saying, "You'd better come down to the studio. Your husband is having an affair with a so-and-so." The same person called up

Sybil Burton several times and said, "I'm sitting in a window at the studio and at the moment I am watching Richard Burton drive Elizabeth Taylor off the studio lot. I think you better do something about it."

But one of the sweetest, wildest moments I've ever had came on that *Cleopatra* set. We were going to shoot Cleopatra's entrance into Rome, and our notoriety had been at full tilt for a couple of months. Five days before the scene, the Vatican had written a most horrific denunciation of me. I had recently adopted little Maria in Germany, and they said I was certainly unworthy to adopt a child. Not only that, I was such a vile human being that my own children should be taken away from me.

So I was going to have to do this scene in front of about five thousand extras, almost all Catholics and probably irate. I was going to be up on that Sphinx all alone with a little boy. Richard and I drove onto the set in the limousine together. We passed three men who made jeering sounds into the car. There had been bomb threats and the Italian equivalent of the FBI were all over the studio. But with five thousand people, how were they going to detect the bloke with the bomb? And what about the rotten tomatoes, the rotten eggs, the rifles—whatever? I suffer terribly from vertigo anyway, and just a five-thousand-people boo would send me toppling off that three-story-high thing.

I panicked and held onto Richard and said, "I don't think I can do it." Richard said, "It's all right, baby, I'll be here and the police are here." I thought, Well, in front of the children and my mother and father I mustn't look afraid. So I got into my costume, which seemed to weigh hundreds of pounds—a huge thing made of twenty-four-karat gold thread. The headdress itself weighed about fifteen pounds and was two and a half feet high. I got the whole drag on and crawled up on the Sphinx, feeling totally trembly.

The extras had been told what they were supposed to do—scream "Cleopatra! Cleopatra!" and wave like mad. Richard was out of the shot but I was supposed to look at him. Mother and Dad and the kids were standing right next to him. Richard had his hand on his dagger—he'd had it sharpened. I don't know what he thought he could do, but he looked ready to sell his life dearly.

So they yelled "Action," and it echoed and ricocheted around the set as men took up the cry—"Action," "Action," "Action"—and the Sphinx started to move. We had to go under a sort of Arc de Triomphe, and the crowd was all waving and they were yelling "Cleopatra! Cleopatra!" I had to be sitting like a Sphinx, not moving, not smiling, doing nothing, staring straight ahead at Caesar with arms folded, holding the emblems of Isis—and not, by the way, trembling. As we got into the dense, thick crowd, the extras started running toward the Sphinx. "Here it comes, Bessie," I thought. Suddenly the chant started changing. It was no longer "Cleopatra." It was "Leeez! Leeez! *Baci! Baci!*" and they were cheering and blowing kisses. The tears were pouring down my face. Richard came running down, Joe Mankiewicz came running down, the cameramen came running down and practically everybody had wet eyes.

In Rome, Richard wouldn't ever let me read what they were saying about us in the newspapers. It was wise, because no matter how much of a façade you put on, it hurts desperately, especially when they add untruths. What used to kill us was when people would say, "We don't care what they do in private life, but do they have to air their dirty laundry in public?" We were doing everything we could not to make it public. I think we went out together maybe five times in all those months—and we ran and the photographers ran after us.

Photographers dressed up like priests used to come to the door; or they'd get inside as workmen or plumbers. Sometimes, outside in the garden, we were besieged by the *paparazzi*. They were on the wall, climbing up with stepladders from the outside. And the servants would come rushing out with brooms and rakes, and the kids turned the hose on those maniacs. And yet we were accused of airing our "little affair" in public.

It seemed like everybody who worked for Richard or me in Rome made a fortune selling their stories to the press. The first servant who went turncoat—long before I met Richard—was the most dignified, charming, very tall Latin maitre d', with a beautifully cut white coat. He had the most magnificent air, and was a would-be artist. I lent him my paint set that cost me $750. He asked me if I would mind posing for him, so occasionally, when I was having dinner in the dining room—Eddie and I alone—he would stand at the other end in his white jacket painting me.

Then all of a sudden the police arrived. I was told he owed thousands of lire in back alimony. I ended up paying what he owed to keep him out of jail, and was all for keeping him on. But everybody advised me against it. When he asked me, though, "Do you mind terribly madam, if I finish the portrait?" I said, "No, not at all, of course you can finish the portrait." He promised he would return the paint set and easel and would give me the painting as a gift.

Well, of course, he just scooted off and, I heard, wrote the most diabolical articles about the activities in the house. On the outskirts of Rome the lights go off approximately every half-hour, so in all the rooms, the bathrooms, everyplace, you have to have tons of candles. There was no mirror in either the bedroom or the bathroom, so I had a mirror installed on the one and only wall where you could see to make sure whether your hems were straight. That happened to be on the other side of the bathtub.

In one of his stories this man is supposed to have said I was so vain that I bathed by candlelight—the proof was that I had candles all around my bathtub. And not only that, I had to have a mirror to watch myself while I was bathing!

The second major-domo I hired did the same thing. I'm told he sold out to an Italian firm of magazines and that he made up a vision so wild it's really kind of funny. He said I used to dress in diaphanous pajamas and, crawling about the floor, would say to him, "Emanuel, don't you think I look like a pussycat?" I must say Elizabeth Taylor in diaphanous pajamas saying to the headwaiter, "Don't you think I look like a pussycat?" —it's a fascinating picture.

A woman whom Richard hired for his children turned out to be a fake Italian countess, and she sold her story in America. Finally, I decided I'd better go to the pantry myself and duel with the rats. God, that was a filthy house. One day the sewer erupted and the whole kitchen was floating in sewage.

The final humiliation was to have to

see *Cleopatra*. The British Embassy trapped me into it. They requested me to take the Bolshoi Ballet as my guests to a screening of *Cleopatra*. I couldn't very well say no. When it was over, I raced back to the Dorchester Hotel and just made it into the downstairs lavatory before I vomited.

I'm being sued by Twentieth Century-Fox and one of their complaints is that when somebody asks me what I think of the film, I tell them. It seems you're not supposed to say what you think. If one can't criticize something one had a part in creating, something's bloody wrong someplace.

I don't think our performances can be judged by the film. The only things I am proud of, Fox cut out with unerring accuracy—namely, the core of the characterization. Richard's part built marvelously from a very strong man with a flaw until you could see him disintegrate. They cut the film so all you see is him drunk and shouting all the time, and you never know what in his character led up to it. He just looks like a drunken sot on campus.

I really could have done without *Cleopatra* except for meeting Richard. I think it was a little like damnation to everybody. Hume Cronyn, when he was told that it was his last shot, was on top of the barge—maybe three stories up. With his gray wig and beard and his sandals and his long smock, he yelled "Hallelujah!" and leaped overboard in the most perfect swan dive.

Hume was the only one who really went out with style. For the rest of us, *Cleopatra* just sort of dribbled off. After my last shot, there was a curiously sad sort of aching, empty feeling—but such astronomical relief. It was finally over. And then it wasn't finally over. Months later I had to go to Paris and do some more. It was like a disease, shooting that film—an illness one had a very difficult time recuperating from.

CHAPTER SEVEN

A S *CLEOPATRA* ENDED, I wrote Richard a letter which said that we were destroying too many lives. We should part. And we did. He went with his family to his house near Geneva. I went to my house in Gstaad in Switzerland. Perhaps I could have gone farther away. But I don't think I lied to myself, because it *was* the only home I had—my children were going to school there. At one time I was tempted to go to America, but I thought, No, that's cowardly; it would be like running away from your loneliness. And Richard was really back with his family in every sense. This was, incidentally, when I decided to divorce Eddie. There was no other way for either of us, even though Richard, I thought, was out of my life.

Gstaad, high on that mountain, is a

141

pretty lonely place out of season. I love being with my children, but I was dying inside and trying to hide it from the children with all kinds of frenzied activity—games, picnics. But they knew—not that I would unburden my problems on their small but steady shoulders. Michael wrote notes—"I know it's going to be all right, Mama." Christopher once said, "I prayed to God last night that you and Richard would be married." That made me cry.

It was like a hair shirt, but I learned for the first time to live totally alone, and not call the police station—my mother and dad, who were staying across the valley—for help. It had always been too easy to find someone to be sympathetic, be angry, give me the answer I wanted. Now with everything frightening, the ramifications horrendous, this was a time to resort to myself, to weigh, to analyze.

Those months there in Switzerland were so full of pain and guilt that they zoom in and out and become all out of shape in my mind. I can remember moments of such horror. And I can remember marvelous moments. After a couple of months Richard called me and asked me to have lunch with him—he was worried about how I was. I had sincerely thought I would never see him again. We were to meet at the Chateau de Chillon on Lake Geneva at two o'clock. My mother and dad came down in the car with me from Gstaad. I was driving along the lake from one direction, and he was driving the other way from Geneva.

We arrived exactly at the same moment. The top of his car was down, he was terribly sun-tanned and his hair was cut very short. I hadn't seen him since *Cleopatra*. I was sitting in the back seat with my parents and he didn't see us right away. He looked nervous, not happy, but so marvelous. His eyes were like bright blue bulbs, and he was looking around. And all of a sudden I got like first-night fear—I couldn't get out of the car. I grabbed one arm of my father and one arm of my mother and I said, "Oh, doesn't he look wonderful? Oh, I don't know what to do, I'm scared." I didn't know how to get out of the car. My mother put her arms around me, and said, "Have a lovely day, baby." My father put his arms around me and kissed me. By that time, he'd seen us and he walked up to the car and said hello kind of shyly. I said hello, and began to stammer. My father gave me a shove, and I got out and we shook hands. Finally, Richard gave me a peck on the cheek. Then Mother and Dad drove off toward Gstaad.

We stood there looking at each other. I had just washed my hair and I had on a brand-new dress. He'd just washed his hair; it was all shiny. And we both said at the same moment, "Well, you look marvelous." And everything we said for about an hour was Chesterfield—you know, at the same moment and the same words. And then there'd be these awful silences when we couldn't say anything. It was like my first date when I was about sixteen, and it was as though he'd never seen a girl before. At last we began to relax and we had lunch at a place overlooking the lake. Then he drove me home. We didn't even kiss.

After that we saw each other maybe once every three weeks or so, usually for lunch. I was always so happy to see him that there was never any talk of the past or of the future. I'd come to my decision—the most alone, mature and unpopular decision of my life. I would be

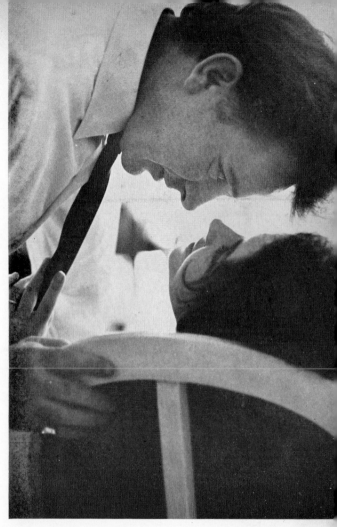

Leaning back in a chair, Elizabeth Taylor pulls Richard Burton down toward her by his necktie. "I am so proud of Richard," she says. "I love not being me, not being Elizabeth Taylor—but being Richard's wife."

While his costumes for *The Sandpiper* are being fitted, Richard Burton entertains, top, with a fascinating flow of conversation. As Elizabeth Taylor joins them, middle, Richard Burton delivers a husbandly "How do you like my new sport coat?" At bottom, in Puerto Vallarta, Mexico, Richard Burton is in his habitual place at the center of attention, telling a story to his wife, at left, and delighted callers. Elizabeth Taylor describes her husband at parties as "always surrounded by layers and layers of people."

On the set of *Cleopatra* in Rome, Elizabeth Taylor discusses with the director, Joe Mankiewicz, how to play a scene they will do later. Left, on the set, she nurses her finger, which she cut accidentally on a prop dagger. Right, she affectionately banters Richard Burton, dressed as Mark Antony.

On the lavish set of *Cleopatra*, Elizabeth Taylor discusses a scene
with Richard Burton between takes.

Rehearsing the banquet scene in *Cleopatra*, Richard Burton, in costume, and Elizabeth Taylor, in street clothes, go through their parts for director Mankiewicz, at right.

In a boyish haircut she gave herself on impulse with a pair of manicure scissors, Elizabeth Taylor, then Mrs. Michael Wilding, holds one-year-old Michael on her lap. Describing those first years as Mrs. Wilding, she says, "It was a lovely, easy life, very simple, very quiet. We didn't do much. We had friends. We raised cats and dogs, read, and worried about money problems. Two babies were born."

Deep in conversation with her sons, above, Elizabeth Taylor listens intently to Michael, left, and Christopher Wilding during a birthday party for her daughter Liza. In picture at left, she gives her full attention to Michael during a party at the closing of Richard Burton's *Hamlet* in New York.

Above, her child who is most likely to go into acting, Elizabeth Taylor's Michael performs the speeches of Puck from Shakespeare's *A Midsummer Night's Dream*. Afterwards, during this family gathering at Elizabeth Taylor's parents' home in Beverly Hills, she proudly and fondly congratulates her son. At bottom, playing with a joke gift at his sister's birthday party, Michael mugs at Roddy McDowall's camera.

Christopher Wilding, blessed with his mother's striking eyes, hugs her dog, a Yorkshire terrier named Thomas à Becket. Describing Christopher, Elizabeth Taylor says, "There's a lot of the typical English schoolboy about him. You know, it's just not done to show emotions."

During a get-together of the Taylor clan, Elizabeth Taylor hitches a ride in a toy trailer with her nephew Tommy, the son of her brother Howard. The gasoline-powered toy tractor, which has Michael at the wheel, was originally a gift to him and Christopher from Michael Todd.

there whenever Richard wanted to call me. I thought, Well, if that's the way it's going to be, that is the role I will accept. Not very satisfying, but it was better than nothing. At least I wouldn't be hurting anybody, and it seemed we really could not stay away from each other.

I guess that before Richard I was somebody who needed to be married—probably because of my basic insecurity, my basic fear. But I loved Richard so much that for the first time it was an unselfish love. I didn't want to marry Richard because I didn't want him to be unhappy. I didn't want Sybil to be unhappy. I would have been perfectly content to just talk to him on the phone every once in a while. I couldn't ever have dated anybody else.

In fact, my nature is not one that can have casual dates. At times, between marriages, I have been pursued. And I don't like that feeling of being pursued en masse. I don't like the idea of going out with ten different guys in a month, flitting like a moth from one superficial friendship or flirtation to another. I just cannot do that round of dressing up and going out to dinner and going to a nightclub and making chitchat with some-

145

body you don't know, somebody that you want to have like you or they want to make you like them.

On the few occasions when I went back briefly into the world, I got a rush of invitations from up-and-coming young actors to take me out. Now, I know it wasn't because of my scintillating personality. It was for publicity reasons. It didn't make me feel bitter, it merely amused me—and of course I didn't go out. I'd rather be alone and read than "date." I'd rather be with my children, wake up early and go to sleep early. And I'm not saying whether that's good or bad. It is probably highly indifferent of me, probably quite stupid. But it's me.

I also refused to play any games to get Richard. Maybe I could have made him want me more if I'd acted unattainable, made him jealous. But it would have been dishonest because I loved him so much. By making myself so readily available, I lowered my stature in everybody's eyes but mine—and, as it turned out, but Richard's.

After several months we both had to go to Paris to do some additional scenes on *Cleopatra*. Richard had already been asked to do *The VIP's*, and I made a joke about "Why don't I do it, too?" The producer grabbed onto it. It really was just an excuse to be together. But even then we weren't together. It was neither one thing nor the other. He couldn't leave his family. We were all there. He's really a very honorable man and he suffered the tortures of the damned.

I know I'm supposed to be a nonconformist, but I really do believe in the laws set up by man—and in God's laws, too. I know it's incongruous for me to say it, but I also don't believe in divorce. But neither did Richard and I believe in what was happening, ten people in limbo suffering so dreadfully. The only way to lessen it was to make a definite move. We did want everything to work out the other way. But it didn't. Everybody's unhappiness had reached a point of no return. And we thought it would have been wrong to make *everybody* keep on paying—*no one* was happy.

There was only one thing good about that long period in limbo. We were put through a time of such—to use a cliche —brimstone and fiery water—oh God, it was awful—that if our love had not been valid, it certainly would have disintegrated and turned into anything from disgust to shame. And it meant that we acted with full knowledge. If we were wrong, no lame excuses. Richard started talking marriage; he had made his decision. Of course, I wanted to be his wife more than anything else in the world.

It was during the rehearsals of Richard's *Hamlet* in Toronto that we went to Montreal and got married. It was like coming home—a golden warmth. We knew then that there was only one way, indirectly, that we could make it up to all the ones who had suffered: by being good to each other and loving each other. And already, out of that wreckage, something good has been born. But it has to be not just for now. In twenty-five years, fifty—then our marriage will have meaning, then all the unhappiness will at least have been *for* something. Maybe if they realize that . . .

For several years before we were married, Richard had felt completely empty, used up as a serious stage actor. He had lost all zest for doing any of the great stage roles again. Then came the offer of *Hamlet*. Richard very sweetly gives me all the credit for his accepting that. And, of course, he broke all the records for the longest run of the play on Broadway, held by Maurice Evans and John Gielgud. Maurice's *Hamlet* was produced by Mike Todd, which gives you an idea how the world can turn full circle before you can turn your back.

I learned in New York that there is no deodorant like success. Richard and I had been called so scandalous we could get very few people on the phone. All of a sudden, after the opening of *Hamlet,* all the people were beaming and sighing. People who hadn't spoken to us in two years were patting him on the back and giving me a kiss on the cheek.

When Richard and I go someplace together where crowds gather, they come across so strong—really raise tidal waves of emotion. It's terribly moving, though it's hard to tell sometimes whether it's antagonism or it's saying, "Never mind, don't worry, we're for you." In Rome there was no doubt. We were spit on there; and going through those crowds I was glad I didn't speak Italian. Sometimes I got so scared I thought I was going to give birth to square eggs.

Traveling to Mexico for Richard to do *Night of the Iguana,* the mob scene in Montreal was unspeakable. There were just the two of us with Liza, and we hadn't bothered to disguise our names. We got out to change planes— Richard was carrying Liza—and suddenly it was mayhem. We got separated and I kept pleading, "Where are my daughter and Mr. Burton?" and they kept pushing microphones at me, awful things on sticks they shove right in your eyes. They'd ask me questions like "Which leading lady do you think Mr. Burton is going to make love to?" Richard was trying to get to me through the crowd, and they had the same sticks in his mouth and asking, "Who is it going to be this time, Sue Lyon or Ava Gardner?" Here he had this child on one arm.

In Boston, when we arrived at the Sheraton-Plaza Hotel for the *Hamlet* tryouts, there were only three policemen, and about three thousand people squashed into that rather small hotel lobby. It was terrifying—one girl had her leg broken—all of the people pressing in to grab and touch. I heard a shrill male voice in back of me shrieking, "See if she has her wig on!" So one of his friends reached up and yanked and found out evidently that it wasn't a wig. But he wanted to make sure, so he went *yank, yank,* and each time my head snapped back. You couldn't even move your arms because of the pressure of the crowd. Then this same effeminate voice screamed, "Get some for a souvenir!" So I had a great glob of hair torn out. And then somebody pulled my shoulder to— you know—"Let's see what she looks like." There was no way of moving an inch in any direction. This somebody kept hauling on my shoulder to corkscrew me around, and all he managed to do was sprain my shoulder.

Finally, the elevator came down. Richard had hold of my hand, although our bodies had become separated and the gap was filled by other human bodies. Then Richard—he was a very good rugby player, thank God—he rammed his way into the elevator, tugging on my hand with both of his. But nobody could give because everybody was fitted tight as a stack of cards. Somebody was again pulling on one arm, and Richard was tugging on the other. I really thought that Richard was going to end up with one half and this stranger would have the remnants of the other half. Finally, the whole tangle sort of fell sideways, and I slid, half-horizontally, to the elevator, trembling.

The crowd that used to gather at the stage door every night at *Hamlet* in New York—I guess there were thousands of people—they came, aside from the rubberneckers, I think partly to pay tribute to Richard as an actor and partly to express friendship. They'd clap for us, you know. And sometimes in restaurants then, people would call out things like, "We're with you. Good luck!" Richard and I are going through a period now, I feel, in which a lot of people are beginning to realize that we're not monsters. Some may even like us for being honest. Some may even have an inkling of what bloody hell it was—that I didn't just bat my eyelashes and Richard batted his, and that was *all* there was to it.

Even at the height of our notoriety, we could go into any ordinary pub in London, and nobody looked around, except maybe to say "Hello, Luv"—and that's very precious to us. It is a big reason why we will probably settle eventually in England—and of course my husband *is* British. My God, we've got to stop moving around so the kids can have one school, one set of friends, have a pony and all their dogs and cats. I'm dying to unpack so I can hang all my paintings, so Richard can put out all his books, so I can have a house to take care of.

And that is why I want to become purely a citizen of Britain, where I was born. It has nothing to do with taxes, which, if anything, are higher in England. But to become British I have to sign a paper which includes the statement that I abjure all allegiance and loyalties to the United States of America. I told them in Paris, "Why should I say that? I don't feel it. I don't mean it. It is a lie—so I am being asked to perjure myself."

I love America. I want to do nothing that might seem ungrateful or might hinder my returning here. But I don't like living in Hollywood. I don't think we'll ever live in New York. And we're certainly not going to live in Kansas City. As it stands now, I don't want to sign the paper as long as that clause is in it.

Richard and Elizabeth as actors and celebrities are going into semiretirement in a few years—I much sooner than Richard. Once you're up there on that last rung, your head splitting in two, you can only go down. I don't want to be pushed off. I want to walk down with all the dignity I can summon—and not with crutches. I think Richard eventually will give up acting to become a serious writer. His writing is much like his conversation—almost like poetry.

I am so proud of Richard. Oh, it's marvelous. He's so total, so complete. I love not being Elizabeth Taylor, but being Richard's wife. I would be quite content to be his shadow and live through him. He has such fun, it's contagious. His relish, his energy—it's like knowing a whirlwind that sparkles and shoots off and people catch the sparkle. He has this mercurial, retentive, darting brain—there's something wild, rather like a running deer, about his thinking.

He's one of the most eloquent talkers in the whole world. A lot of people think he can do it off the bat, that he was born with his mouth open and that it's never been shut since. But he is not a huge extrovert. He's got this terrible shyness, and nobody knows the pangs, the sort of death throes, that he goes through. In order to become an extrovert he really has to have a couple of drinks.

He remembers things from when he was four years old, can tell you anecdotes as if he had written them all out ahead of time. Always the longer word is better and more fun to roll around. He was an actor even when he was just a little puddle. Sometimes when his father came home in a temper or stoned or something, his brothers would go get Richard, who was a fat, cherubic child and had a wicked sense of humor. They would sit him up on the table and tell him to sing and dance, and he would charm the old man into a good mood. He was age one when they started doing that, and he hasn't stopped. My name for him is Charlie Charm.

And he's such a perverse tease. Nothing delights him more than to call me, in front of some reporter, "A comfy, nice little girl," and then throw in something about double chin and stumpy legs, and then end with, "She has breakfast like any normal person. There are times when she's so normal I'm tempted to leave her."

The two of us act like we're seventeen-year-olds. My favorite time is when we're alone at night and for hours we giggle— and talk—about, maybe, books, world events, poetry, the children, when we first met, problems, daydreams, real dreams. We love to watch bad old movies on TV to regenerate our souls. Sometimes I wake up in the morning with my eyes absolutely swollen shut from crying at some wonderfully awful movie the night before. I remember one that was about an old man and old woman who had given birth to five kids. The old couple had had a farm and lost the farm. Although all the children turned out well-to-do, none of them would take the parents both together because they found them old-fashioned and boring. How I cried over that one.

As a matter of fact, even our fights are fun—nothing placidly bovine about us. Richard loses his temper with true enjoyment. It's beautiful to watch. Our fights are delightful screaming matches, and Richard is rather like a small atom bomb going off—sparks fly, walls shake, floors vibrate.

I heard about some people who were staying in New York at the Regency Hotel and who deliberately got the suite below ours. Can you believe this? They hired it almost a month in advance, and they stood up on several chairs and put empty glasses against the ceiling and listened to what was going on. Well, they got an earful. I think the glasses cracked, and they went around telling everybody, "Oh, it's terrible, it's a shame about the Burtons. Oh, we heard the most awful fight." But what the poor schmoes didn't know is that it's a vocal exercise really, that's all.

Once I had the flu, so I was in bed watching television and Richard came in, after *Hamlet,* slightly crocked and in a fury about something. I thought it was because I was sick in bed, because he really can't bear sickness. He said, "Turn that censored, censored television off." And I said, "Oh, but I'm watching the most marvelous movie." I'd never seen Peter Sellers in a movie before and I was really enjoying it and he stalked out of the room. He came back in his pajamas and his bare feet and said, "I was booed tonight," and I said, "Oh, darling, it's just some idiot. Don't pay any attention to that." And I guess I didn't even look at him. And he said, "I was *booed* tonight." And I said, "Don't be so silly."

He sort of tore over to the television set and kicked it right over and it hit the wall and one of the knobs fell off. That wasn't good enough, so he had to kick it on the floor and he kicked quite a large metal screw and cut his foot to the bone.

I put some iodine on it and bandaged it, but at the moment all I could do was really get kind of convulsive. I started laughing and, of course, that's the worst thing you can do. He was in terrible pain. The blood was squirting out all over everything because, you know, he has slight hemophilia and he bleeds quite profusely. And I was helpless with laughter. I think he could have killed me for that.

In our fights and discussions—and some of them are red hot—neither of us ever swears at each other because then it becomes ugly. But I love four-letter words. They're so terribly descriptive, they just give me a good feeling. Richard says they only show a weakness of vocabulary. I've promised not to use them if he will stop telling lies to jazz up his stories.

I never mind being wrong with Richard, because I learn from him and he never treats me like an idiot. He makes me feel an intellectual equal of his, which of course I'm not. And because I don't feel driven to keep pace with him—can just revel in him—I end by keeping up with him in a way.

Richard and I would not be married if it hadn't been for my marriage with Mike. I would not have known, first of all, how to cope with Richard. I probably still am very selfish, but not nearly as selfish as I would have been. It's Mike's great legacy to me—the gift of love—knowing not only how to give, but knowing how to receive with love so the other person feels he has a purpose. Before, I would have been preoccupied with my own idiosyncrasies, my problems, my difficulties. I probably would have expected Richard to adjust to me.

What I mean is that I want terribly to please, not to be pleased. And I have found that when you are not concerned with your own satisfaction or pleasure—only with giving—then you yourself receive so much more. When I please Richard, there is nothing in the world that makes me happier.

And I think Richard loves to please me. Sometimes Richard wakes me up in the middle of the night because he wants to talk to me, or drives an hour out to location when he doesn't have to work, just to say hello. Those times I *"kvell"* —that's a Jewish word for feeling all kind of melted and whipped cream inside.

Richard gave me the most expensive piece of jewelry I have—my engagement pin. It's an emerald as big as a pond, and I love to look into the depth of it. Waves of color . . . green like the middle of the ocean. There's something so pure about stones. It isn't the acquisition, I just love looking at them.

The first time I went to a command performance and met the Queen Mother, I was sixteen and had bronchitis and a high fever. I had to talk my mother into letting me go. We were all in a line and when the Queen Mother got to me, I had to take her hand and go into a deep drop curtsy. And I was so rocky from the temperature I almost toppled over, and my heel got caught in the hem of my dress, which was a long chiffon thing. I was sort of kneeling there, literally hanging onto her hand to keep from falling, when my eyes caught hold of and fastened onto her necklace. I never looked at her face at all. This terrible expression came on my face and somebody from *Life* magazine clicked a photograph and they ran it with a suitable comment. I almost died of shame. You've never seen such avarice—my eyes out on stalks.

Richard doesn't like to give presents when you're supposed to give presents.

Christmas and birthdays go right by. But when he goes out and buys something, say, because it's a Tuesday, he's terribly excited. He pretends he isn't and gets all sort of "Okay, goddamnit, take it." But you can see he's stepping from one foot to the other and he smokes six cigarettes in two minutes and ends up with one in each hand. And he can't quite force down his smile, but it begins to come up every once in a while.

I would be unspeakably smug not to realize that in happy marriages, during a sort of middle-aged change of life, men do flit around with young, pretty girls. But if Richard and I ever went through such a time, whatever will be called for to keep our marriage together I think I will have the guts and the compassion to do. I would love him enough to love the hurt he might give me and be patient. I have learned that pride is very bad, the kind of pride that makes you say, "I won't tolerate that."

I really, profoundly believe that no such thing will *ever* happen. There is no question, of course, with me, and Richard I believe totally—with my guts, with my soul. The longer we are married, the more our faith and trust are deepening, the more our relationship is tightening. We've gone through so many intimate things together, learned so much! We are so aware that our responsibility is not just to us, Elizabeth and Richard. It's to all the people we have ever hurt.

And I do realize that we are both mercurial, jealous people. I am jealous of his past, of the women he knew before me. When I see one, something happens to me inside. But I know intellectually that it's irrational and stupid and *my* problem. Since I first met Richard, he has never given me a single jealous moment.

Every so often I get an extraordinary feeling about Richard—once, for instance, on shipboard when he was walking through the dining room toward me, again during a party when he was mesmerizing a bunch of people. I sort of detached myself, as though I was floating upward and looking down with great clarity on the two of us—like in a Chagall painting. Then a shock, a thrill goes through my body. I really feel all strange and goose-bumpy. It's, I don't know, maybe the pride of possession, the pride of love. He looks so bloody handsome.

Now to have found, through trial and error, a tranquillity in proud subordination to somebody else—it is so beautiful. I have been working since the age of ten and I'm afraid I was too strong and willful at times. I must have been awful to live with because I have always wanted to be independent. Indeed, I always *have* been independent, even though I knew I wanted more than anything else in the world a man who could control me. I have found that man. I don't get away with nuttin'.

As I've said, I used to test Mike, but I have no need for that with Richard. A little example: We were going to dinner and I was puttering around—I hadn't showered or anything. Richard said, "Listen, Luv, I'm leaving this house in exactly twenty minutes, so if you're going with me, get your drag on and come." In eighteen minutes flat I'd had my bath, put on my make-up and was sitting in the living room saying, "Hee, hee, I've got time for a drink."

And Richard pays all the bills. That's only happened in my life once before. I think it must be terrible for a man if his wife is . . . well, I know what it can do. Both sides lose respect. When I finally started making big money, which was with *Suddenly Last Summer,* I was absolutely broke. I'd loaned it all. And since then—until I married Richard—almost everything was spent.

Nowadays the money I earn goes mainly into trusts for the children. For some reason I feel kind of apologetic about costing somebody a million dollars for a picture. It is still like a dream. I still can't believe it—especially when I never *see* it, and especially when people would be flabbergasted to know how little of my pay ever becomes mine. But a million does seem like such a crazy amount to pay for anybody to do anything. I guess it's just part of the weirdness of the moving picture industry.

Also, inadvertently, I have created a kind of exclusivity for myself. By not being consumed by ambition, I can wait for the films I really want to do, for whatever reasons—including monetary ones. And I am a bit proud of the fact that evidently nobody has ever lost a dime on any picture I have made. And that includes *Cleopatra,* too.

Richard and I know our present high living can't possibly last, so we're trying to be more sensible. Richard has me on a clothing allowance, and I take such a delight in keeping to it. I used to really throw money around in the years before I met Richard. The way some women do when they're depressed—you know, go out and buy a hat—I used to go out and spend a fortune at Dior's, just on a ripping, go-to-hell tear. I didn't even enjoy the clothes—gave a lot of them away.

One of the biggest changes in my way of living is that before Richard I'm afraid I was a bit of a slob. After Mike died, I used to sleep fourteen, fifteen hours a day—I think mainly to avoid what the waking hours would bring. Who was it who called sleep "a little death"? Now I go along on five or six hours of sleep. I think that's very symptomatic.

My God, I was on a merry-go-round for so long. Now I've stopped spinning and, oh, the relief to be able to breathe and look and think and feel without panic. I'm not afraid of myself. I'm no longer afraid of what I will do. I have absolute faith in our future. Richard has given me all this.

CHAPTER EIGHT

THROUGHOUT EVERYTHING, my children have been the one consistently bright spot in my life. I've always loved kids. I don't mean I love *all* kids. I'm not one of those people who go up to a baby and sort of tweak its cheek and say, What a sweet, gootchy baby.

Needless to say, it was vitally important to me how they reacted to Richard. During *Cleopatra* we played it terribly carefully in front of the children, and never behaved with each other as anything other than friends. But, of course, they must have sensed something because they're so intelligent, so absolutely tuned in. After a while they started asking, "When is Richard coming over?" Michael, I think, was the first one to come around, and then Liza. Christopher was not actively hostile, but he was just another little person in front of Richard. He would shake hands with him. But before we were married, and really noticeably since we've been married, Christopher began to throw himself into Richard's arms and kiss him.

When we were in Switzerland and everything between me and Richard seemed to be over, their sense of loss was almost as bad as mine. It is wonderful they felt that way, but at that time I didn't know what to do. I tried to explain to them that Richard had little girls that he loved, that he loved my kids as well, but his obligation was to his family. They were very sweet about it, but they couldn't figure out why he couldn't love us all.

Now, of course, they're absolutely certain that Richard and I will always be married. He's the absolute boss of the household and they respect him for that. Up until Richard, I was the only person they would go to with their problems. At the same time, Richard's humor breaks them up. He becomes completely the same age as the kids, maybe even younger, and he's so physically active he can wear them out. When we're all together, alone, we sound like Martians, and switch the game maybe ten times an hour—becoming different people, creatures, saying goofy things.

No matter how superficial or ridiculous the game might be, Richard is teaching them the whole time. And they love it. He's already told them all the Shakespearean classics. It can take him an hour and a half sometimes to stage one, acting out all the parts, reciting some of the verse. They sit absolutely rapt and then try to make him do it all over again.

I think it's pretty clear that Michael will eventually become an actor. He is already memorizing Shakespeare. And you know something? He has talent. He has been offered several chances in films, but we have absolutely refused. An *ex*-child actress in the family is enough—too much maybe.

Michael is terribly deep and sensitive, and it takes him a long time to grow fond of somebody—but then he's a wonderful friend. He writes me loving little notes all the time, takes great time over them—things he'd blush and stammer over if he had to say them to me. I still blush; it runs in the family. He's almost a teen-ager now and just this year has all of a sudden grown up. On the ship when we came over to do *Who's Afraid of Virginia Woolf?,* Michael had his first girl friend, and all sorts of sweet things began going on. One day she whispered, "Michael, when am I going to see you again?" and he answered, under his breath, out of the side of his mouth, "Ping-pong, tomorrow."

Christopher, who is two years younger and worships Michael, was absolutely excluded. Michael said things like, "All right, you can come to the movies, but sit way, way away from us." Christopher is quite gregarious and a bit of a clown and he really is as sweet as he looks. But there's a lot of the typical little English schoolboy about him. It's just not done to show emotions, though maybe his are deeper than any of the other children's. Just sitting next to you is terribly important to him. If Christopher takes hold of your hand, it makes you tingle. In his funny, quiet way, a squeeze of the hand speaks volumes. Sometimes Christopher will come over and very quietly put his hand on Richard's arm and say something terribly serious. And Richard will answer it as though he were answering his professor when he went to Oxford.

170

We taught Chris, who loves bugs, to say "lepidopterist," and that's what he tells patronizing grownups who ask what he's going to be when he grows up. The expression on their faces!

Liza is a sort of an independent tornado. She takes charge of the boys. She takes charge of Richard. I gave up the day she was born. She looks so much like Mike—her mannerisms, the way she uses her hands, the way she shrugs her shoulders—and the larceny and con of her mind. It gives you the creeps; she was only seven months old when Mike was killed. At one time the resemblance could make me run from the room crying. It was Mike. The only thing missing was a cigar.

Of course, Liza knows all about Mike and what a marvelous man he was. She has a great sense of pride in him. We showed *Around the World in Eighty Days* in Dublin. She was thrilled to see his name up on the screen, and know that this was her real daddy's picture. Sometimes she does call Richard Daddy. But he would never say, "I'm not Daddy —call me Richard." It happens because of her sense of belonging, I think. She knows exactly that Richard is her step-

171

father and she has a marvelous teasing rapport with him.

Peter O'Toole, who pretends he cannot bear other people's children, dogs or cats, was playing one day with Liza and being absolutely enchanting. They were chatting away like two adults around a tea table—or, rather, with Peter O'Toole, on bar stools. Richard said, "Hey, what's up? I thought you hated children." And he said, "Look, I'm no fool. I'm trying to get in good with her, because in twenty years we're all going to have to go to her for jobs. She'll own the industry."

She is totally feminine—a terrible flirt. I asked her what she wanted to be and she said a bride. She'll make somebody a devastating wife. And I wish him luck. Just good luck, wherever you are.

There's something quite untamed about her face—like a little jungle bush-baby. And those eyes. She has a way of looking so directly into your eyes that you feel she is penetrating your brain, as though she knows all the secrets. When she was a few months old, she would look at people through the bars of her crib and you could see them cringe, begin to loosen their collars and loosen their ties, sort of shift their shoulders.

You would think she'd hate discipline, but it gives her security. She does the same thing I did when I was a kid. When I was spanked, I withdrew and became like inside an oyster shell. The punishment didn't penetrate. But if I were spoken to and made to realize that I'd done something naughty, oh, I'd be so ashamed of myself.

She's interested in everything that the boys do. She's mad for animals. She picks up anything stray—stray children, all stray people, all stray animals, anything slightly wounded. She's terribly like me in that sense. It is not true that I like animals more than people. But they come a very close second. There is no bull about them. With one tilt of a Siamese cat's chin, with its terrible sort of butterfly eyes, it accepts you or it doesn't.

Liza is very protective and motherly toward Maria. It's so sweet, because it's kind of old-fashioned. When Maria spills something on her dress or whatever, it's "Now, Maria, you really mustn't do that, dear." That attitude.

Maria's adoption is now completed

and her legal name is Maria Burton. When I woke up from my close call with Liza, I found the doctors had put me out of commission for having any more children of my own. But I've always wanted a big family. During *Cleopatra*, with the help of Maria Schell, I found this little Maria in Germany. She was nine months old, covered with abscesses, suffering from malnutrition, had a crippled hip that was going to cripple her for life—and I just loved her. She didn't cry, she didn't laugh, she was in a laundry basket with two pillows stuffed in the bottom. She had very dark eyes. She watched everything, and I held her and I bathed her and I changed her for three days and finally she started giggling, and finally she would cry when she wanted her bottle.

This funny little introverted person that was just sort of half-asleep responded so much to love—the warmth, I think, of two arms. Anyway, I was hooked by the end of a few days. The German officials wanted me to have a "perfect baby," so I had to fight like a tiger to get her. To me she *was* perfect.

I took her to doctors in Germany, Italy, France. She was spread-eagled in a cast for about two years, and we really didn't know whether she would walk ever. Finally, a man at Oxford, a great doctor, advised an operation to put in a metal plate. Now she can even run and has begun to speak. Her first word was "Mama." I guess that's universal, but when it happens, you just die.

While we were in New York during *Hamlet,* the German adoption authorities came over to investigate us to be certain we would give Maria a good home. They were dying to see *Hamlet.* When Richard came to the "To be or not to be" soliloquy, he delivered the first lines in German. It was electrifying, and the German investigators flipped.

While we were all in Paris during the filming of *The Sandpiper,* we had an awful experience connected with Maria. We'd come back from the studio, and we always used to have one drink in the lounge of the Lancaster Hotel before we went upstairs to have dinner and go to bed. My back was to the door, and a young man, a young woman and a stout, elderly-looking woman rushed in, and the young woman pushed the stout woman right up against my chair. The young man fired off a flashbulb and then raced off. It all happened in a matter of seconds.

The two women said something in German. Richard and I looked at each other and in unison said to the young woman, "Is that Maria's mother?" And she said, "Yes. I'm a great friend of hers and I'm going to interpret for her." I guess then I got bug-eyed with outrage. "You're no friend of hers," I screamed. "You're a journalist and get out of here before I kill you!" And she said, "I *am* a friend of hers—I'm a *great* friend of hers and I'm working as her interpreter." Then I said very softly, "Get out of here." Richard let out a few bellows and she left.

I took hold of Maria's mother's arm and asked her to sit down. The poor woman was shaking. I patted her arm and asked if she wanted a drink or something but she didn't understand my English. Fortunately, our lawyer, Aaron Frosch, was coming by the hotel to say good-bye and he speaks Yiddish and a bit of German. He translated enough to say that we were terribly sorry and didn't want to upset her. Then the whole story came out. The two other people were from one of those awful yellow

Presiding over the day's fishing, Richard Burton benignly teases the children who in turn delight in him. "Their love of Richard is so gratifying, really awe-making," says Elizabeth Taylor on the subject of her children and her husband. "His humor breaks them up. He becomes completely the same age as the kids, maybe even younger, and he's so physically active he can wear them out."

Richard Burton, resting up from his record-breaking run of *Hamlet*, follows Liza's pensive gaze during a fishing expedition off Puerto Vallarta, Mexico, where the Burtons own a house.

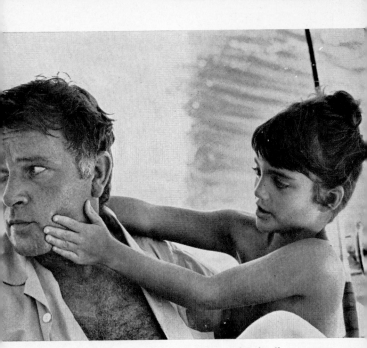

Elizabeth Taylor describes Liza Todd—at right, fondly torment-
ing Richard Burton—as "an independent tornado. She looks so
much like Mike—her mannerisms, the way she uses her hands,
the larceny and con of her mind—that it gives you the creeps."

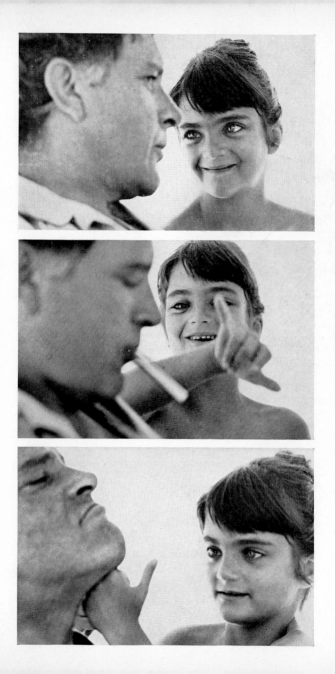

Above, left, at the Puerto Vallarta house, Richard Burton plays "fish" with Liza, and below, he swims with the children near where his movie *Night of the Iguana* was filmed.

In an artist's studio-home built for the film *The Sandpiper* near Monterey, California, all their children visit the Burtons between camera takes. And, mother-henning them, Elizabeth Taylor tells the two girls—Maria, her adopted daughter, left, and Liza—to take it a little easy on her husband as they climb on him. At center, rear, is John Springer, who screens and negotiates all of the Burtons' contacts with the press.

Maria Burton, the German girl whom Elizabeth Taylor adopted
in 1960, combs her mother's hair on the set of *The Sandpiper*.
Below, she plays with a bunch of flowers. Born with a crippled
hip, Maria now, after surgery, can even run with ease.

magazines in France. They had gone to the little tiny village of those poor people, Maria's parents, and said that Richard and I had invited them to come to Paris to see Maria. If they did come, they would be paid by the magazine, and possibly could get money from us. We did not give them any money and they went back to Germany the next day. They were very simple people and, I think, very nice people.

They'd evidently been there for almost a week. When the children had gone out during the day, the photographer had tried to take a picture of Maria in the Rolls-Royce—while, in the background, the mother and father looked longingly at their lost daughter whom they'd given away when she was three days old. And the magazine wanted a picture of the mother standing near the opulence of the Rolls-Royce, her tattered coat contrasting with my fur coat—you know, a little woman standing out in the cold, waiting for days on end to get a look at her child. Fortunately, they didn't get any of the pictures. But how cruel to use those poor people that way.

The children at the time didn't know about this, but I do worry about the effect of my fame on them. I once asked my kids if they would like it better if I weren't in films and weren't famous. Unanimously, they said, "No, we're terribly proud of you."

The boys have a marvelous out that they told me about. Sometimes when snotty kids ask them if their mother is Elizabeth Taylor, they say no and walk away. "We're telling the absolute truth," they told me. "Your name is Elizabeth Burton."

When they went to school in Rome and the other kids did know that I was their mother, they came home, both of them, with a couple of black eyes because the kids had said, "Oh, your mother's a big, fat movie star and she's got big bosoms"—things like that. So whoever said that was socked. The first time it occurred, Michael came home with a fairly bleedy nose. I asked him what happened, and he didn't want to tell me because it would hurt my feelings. About two days later Christopher did tell me. He said, "Boy, you should have seen Michael. Boy, he really flattened that kid!"

I think my children are remarkable people. Each one is so individual, so different. At the same time they're like me —the shyness of the two boys, Liza's temper. It's a combination of her father's and mine, and that's a pretty wild combination. They all have a slight streak of stubbornness, which I have a very large streak of. They all have my eyes—especially the red part. And they're remarkable, too, because, God knows, according to all the rules my life should have been murder for them. Their lives have been up and down. We've lived like gypsies.

And, well, there's the obvious. I've been married too many times. How terrible to change children's affiliations, their affections—to give them the insecurity of placing their trust in someone when maybe that someone won't be there next year. I was terrified that they would stop giving themselves to any man.

My divorce from Michael Wilding was, as I've said, friendly, and the boys see a lot of their father. They're very close to him. They loved Mike Todd. Of course, they couldn't understand his death. In a way, I think it was almost like a betrayal and they didn't know how to cope with it. With Eddie, I was very lucky. They liked him as a friend, but when Eddie left, they didn't even ask where he had gone. They seemed to be much happier, much more relaxed, once that awful, heavy, humid, before-the-storm atmosphere had left the house and left their lives. And, as far as I know, whenever they do think of Eddie, they probably think of him with affection. I hope they do. Now their love of Richard is so gratifying, really awe-making. And through everything *I've* always been there, the one constant thing.

To my kids I'm not Elizabeth Taylor at all; I'm not anybody other than "Mommie." Michael and I were once walking along the street in Puerto Vallarta. He said, "Mommie, everybody's looking at you because you're so pretty." I thought that was so sweet, so dear. He *really can* believe that. He didn't know yet that I was an oddity, some kind of a side show. They still don't know that a lot of people loathe my guts.

CHAPTER NINE

RICHARD AND I hadn't done any serious acting together, nothing that's demanded anything of us, since *Cleopatra*. And you can't really call that very serious.

After we did *VIP's* I didn't get a film offer for what seèmed like ages and ages. Richard and I were both panicky. I think our notoriety was a factor, but not a large one. More important were all the accusations about *Cleopatra*. The industry was convinced that we had cost *Cleopatra* extra millions by caprice—all of which we have proven to be false. And I couldn't get health insurance. So we were risks. I didn't think I could get a job. So I grabbed *Sandpiper* and let them pay their million dollars.

A lot of people, because the plot involves an illicit romance between a bohemian artist and a minister, may think that *Sandpiper* was written specifically for Richard and me in order to capitalize on our notoriety. I did feel it necessary to see a rough cut and take out anything so pertinent to us that I would just die. Actually, the script had been knocking around for several years, and at first they didn't ask Richard to be in it. Then, I had to talk him into doing it. We never thought it would be an artistic masterpiece.

In *Sandpiper* I did a scene—very reluctantly—in which for a split second I'm nude to the waist but covering myself with my hands so it's actually about as nude as a low halter neck. When I did the scene, I had somebody standing in front of me with a towel while I covered myself with my hands. I turned puce from head to foot. I won't even go swimming in a bathing suit in front of strangers, that's how much of an exhibitionist I am.

I think nude scenes in films are absurd, and I think it's really strange the way women, respectable women, will strip for magazines. The ones who don't need the money—it can only be a narcissistic complex, a vanity of the body so profound that they must show it. Or maybe they're just naïve and think it will help their careers.

The one exception was Marilyn Monroe. She needed the money, probably, and she seemed to have a kind of unconscious glow about her physical self that was innocent like a child. When she posed nude it was "Gee, I am kind of, you know, sort of dishy," like she enjoyed it without being egotistical.

I think the whole trend is a comment on the morals of the world—just a bit more, a bit further. The language in films, the language on television, certainly in plays, has become racier. If you don't write four-letter words in, you are considered square.

In *Sandpiper* we were playing two people in love, so it was not particularly difficult. I must say, when we looked at each other, it was like our eyes had fingers and they grabbed hold, and perhaps something special did happen.

Now we have done the film version of Edward Albee's *Who's Afraid of Virginia Woolf?*, a real blockbuster. Richard and I went through a whole set of qualms over taking the roles. Let's face it, we were not obvious casting and a lot of people hooted at the idea. For me, the age thing was wrong. I had never played a part like that. I couldn't imagine myself as Martha, and I couldn't imagine myself dominating Richard. It was the most difficult part I had ever read and made me feel as though in my whole life I'd never acted, never interpreted a line. Then I thought, Well, you never did know how to act. Then I thought, Well, you did a couple of things that were all right, and you felt the same way then. And, of course, no actress could ever turn that role down.

We got word to Albee that we wanted to know what his feelings were before we said yes or no. Albee was terribly sweet. He said he was absolutely delighted and if he could ever be of any help, he would be more than happy.

I never saw *Virginia Woolf* on the stage and I haven't listened to the record. It was done so brilliantly, from what I hear, that it probably would have given me even more of an inferiority complex than I already had. I wanted to create my own Martha who had nothing to do with anybody else's Martha. I think she is a desperate woman who has the softness of the underbelly of a baby turtle. She covers it up with the toughness of the shell, which she paints red. Her veneer is bawdy; it's sloppy, it's slouchy, it's snarly. But there are moments when the facade cracks and you see the vulnerability, the infinite pain of this woman inside whom, years ago, life almost died but is still flickering.

Mike Nichols, the director, and Ernie Lehman, the producer, decided I should be about forty-five. And then we did eight different make-ups, and we all chose the same one. I liked it immediately. Once I got all the trappings on, Martha just happened without anybody discussing it, without my even thinking much about it.

In the wardrobe tests, assuming Martha, taking her on gradually, it was the walk that happened first. I can't describe it. It's a state of mind; it's Martha's walk. Then came the voice. It's in a much lower key than my own, much more bawdy, much more raucous. I've done something with my accent, I don't know exactly what. The hardest thing was the laugh. Martha's laugh is mostly vulgar. There are only one or two times that she laughs genuinely, from inside, and that's quite a different one.

It was very exciting. I had to keep on generating other things every day, because in the film as the evening wears on, there is the drunkenness, the disintegration. It's not static. Martha goes slowly down until at the end there is a new, different element in both Martha and her husband, George. It's like a patient's chart in a hospital.

Though it was such a hard part, because it was such a complete change from anything else, it was strangely one of the easiest things I've ever done. It was stepping into somebody else's skin who was so remote from my own skin that it was like wearing a mustache and beard and old long wig and cloak. So I had Martha to hide behind, so I'd lost Elizabeth Taylor. There was a freedom that I've never known before in a role. I felt much more experimental. Ultimately, of course, I'm not a schizophrenic, so there may have been some of me that came across, but not consciously or, I hope, even subconsciously. I tried to cut all of me out. When I got into my Martha suit, I forgot me.

Take swearing. Until I was curbed by Richard, I used to curse in an almost deliberately kittenish way to shock people;

to watch their reaction. There's nothing cute about Martha at all. When she swears, it's for real. Martha swears in anger. I try never to swear in anger. And Martha doesn't swear to shock people, because the whole consistency of Martha is one vast swear word, one blasphemy.

During the first few weeks of shooting, Martha completely took me over. When I left the set, I couldn't take off my Martha suit. Richard and I would be out with friends and I'd hear myself saying to him, "For Chrissakes, shut up. I'm not finished talking." And then the next morning I would think, That wasn't me, it was Martha. I had to fight to regain myself. Richard totally became George. When I screamed at him, he would still be George—George at the beginning of the film—patient, stoic, likeable. But as we got more into the film, discovered more who George and Martha were, the easier they were to shed. I guess it's like going to a psychiatrist. The more you begin to understand your problem, the more you can leave it behind. And we could be more secure about abandoning our roles because we got more confident that we could step back into them. But it was wild for a month.

If what turned out on film wasn't right, it was still the best I could do. Whether the final product is good or bad, the public will ultimately decide. But I've never been so happy doing a film. It was so marvelous to have those words to say. It was the first character part I've ever played. It was my first part with comedy in it. That's part of the total devastation of the play—that it is a tragicomedy. I mean you go in instants from extreme height to extreme depth— the play throws you around the room like a squash ball. It all had to be rat-a-tat-tat and firecrackers. You couldn't pause, or sort of go "Ah" and look like you're thinking. You started with the trombone. I feel I did it with all holds unbarred.

When Richard and I suggested Mike Nichols as director, everybody fell down in horror because he had never made a film. Then when he got so many hits on Broadway, they were dying to say yes. I think Mike Nichols is a great director. He is so inventive and has this peculiar, bizarre mind that sees only things that he can see. He comes up with far-out ideas, some so minutely detailed that maybe the audience won't even have time to catch them, but which mean so much to you as an actor.

Like when I opened the icebox door in one scene. In front of me in that icebox I discovered a complete portrait of the total disorder of Martha's mind and Martha's life—and Mike had personally chosen and arranged everything. He had an ear of corn, all chewed and put away. There was a tangle of leftover spaghetti on a plate. A can of beans had been opened and left completely full, with the lid folded back. The icebox was packed with things like that. And in the scene I eat a leg of chicken and take the bone and stick it back in the icebox. Now the audience probably notices little of this, but it is all so important to stimulate the total of your performance.

Mike is a hinting director, which makes you get all excited and start inventing and participating in his inventions. That's where he's so wise. He gives you freedom. But at the same time he's the only director I know who has memorized the entire script and quietly feeds you your line if you dry up. He's one of the most brilliant and nicest people I've ever known. And of course, we don't have to talk about his humor.

It is very exciting to me that I have done *Virginia Woolf* with Richard. Well, he is my favorite actor. You have that feeling of antenna—the quivering contact. But also you have that feeling of the absolute pro snapping to. There's none of the self-indulgence that so many actors wallow in. Before a scene they may jump up and down and shake their hands and hold their head and have to work themselves up into a state. In a matter of seconds Richard's emotion is there like a volcano about to erupt—but under his own control.

He never acts the big star. He does things, such as—well, suppose somebody is having trouble with lines and Richard sees that look of panic in the other actor's eyes. Richard will fluff his own line or knock something over—anything so the cut in the film will be his fault. He can remember the agony of being a supporting actor responsible for garbling a line, or missing a mark or a cue. Nerves are the nemesis of all actors, and Richard will do anything at his own expense to put other actors at their ease.

There *are* actors who won't help you at all. This has happened to me so many times. Say, in a highly charged scene, the close-up is of me. The actor, off camera, has to read me an emotional speech, and I have to react to it silently on camera. Many actors or actresses will read it to you absolutely flat—won't give anything for you to react to.

If I'm an actress at all, if I have any technique at all, it must be concentration. Trying to be inside the skin of the person, totally disregarding one's self, trying to become *them,* takes tremendous concentration. And if I am portraying something emotional in a scene, I sweat real sweat and I shake real shakes.

Perhaps I can illustrate my approach using a sweet thing Mickey Rooney did. The first time I ever had to cry was in *National Velvet.* The horse was supposed to have colic, and of course he was Velvet's life. The scene was like a montage, covering the whole night—Velvet putting towels on him and hot water and rubbing him down, putting liniment on him. Finally, when the character Mickey played said he didn't think the horse would live, then Velvet cries.

I knew the scene and it hadn't worried me in the slightest because in those days I could summon up a few tears that would trickle down—but nothing like

Margaret O'Brien. To watch her absolutely fascinated me. It was like turning on faucets—I mean, the tears would come and it made Niagara Falls look ridiculous. And then the faucets would turn off and she'd come bouncing off the set.

Anyway, we rehearsed the scene and Mickey put his arm around me and said, "Honey, you know in this scene you have to cry." And I said, "Yes, Mickey, I know." "Well," he said, "you should think that your father is dying and your mother has to wash clothes for a living, and your little brother is out selling newspapers on the street and he doesn't have shoes and he's cold and shivering, and your little dog was run over." It was like Chekov gone nuts and it was meant to make me start to cry.

Instead, I started to laugh, and I don't know what Mickey thought. Maybe he thought it was hysteria setting in. I didn't have the heart to say anything to him. I tried to control my giggles, but the more I tried, the more I couldn't stop them. When I did the scene, instead of imagining my father drunk and dying and my mother doing laundry in a snow stream, all I thought about was the horse being very sick and that I was the little girl who owned him. And the tears came. But how generous of Mickey to try to help me.

There are so many different schools of acting—and, of course, there is the Method. Those actors transplant themselves into a personal experience that they can identify with. That seems a bit like cheating. I think if you are playing a part, you should not react the way you personally would react; you should react the way the character would react. In *Virginia Woolf* I'm fortunately not very much like my role of Martha. At least not yet. So it can't be Elizabeth Taylor reacting. I have to think how Martha would react. But to give it the breath of reality, the characterization has to bounce from Martha back into some core of my emotional set-up. Ultimately Martha must well up from the deep of my emotions.

So I have to have a more fully stocked reservoir of emotions than the lady from Pismo Beach. That's part of the rip and tear of being an actor. Because to survive in your personal life, you must build up the oyster-shell layers. In acting, however, you have to tear them away. You can't afford layers of self-control.

Actors' emotions must be instantly tappable at the word "action." You have to learn the whole keyboard of your emotions, the limitations and the heights. So there has to come a time when you've been fooling around so much with your nervous system for make-believe that it becomes a bit cracky. And then you might become just slightly "temperamental."

I think most people who are artistic or creative—artists, musicians, actors—have something a little strange. If they were the absolute norm, they wouldn't be doing what they're doing. All the really interesting playwrights don't see things quite normally. And certainly painters don't either. It's that taint that gives them a little vision. You have to have a slight kink to interpret something a bit better than the average, more than the obvious.

While you're doing any film, moments come when you're all keyed up and you've done a take at high, high pitch, high C—and then you have to stop and wait for forty-five minutes while they set up for the next take. That's one place the concentration comes in. During that forty-five minutes you have to stay revved up for the coming take, and keep alive the emotions you had in the last one, and at the same time talk and joke and be yourself. If film acting is an art—and I believe it is—that is part of it. When everything is interruption, you cannot allow yourself to be disturbed or thrown.

What you do is put on another kind of act. So you become all acts within acts, characters within characters. You yourself tend to get lost for a while in something as emotional, as demanding and as hideous, as *Virginia Woolf.*

I think film acting can be an art, and certainly the camera can move in and grab hold of your mind—so the emotion has got to be there behind your eyes, behind your heart. You can never act superficially and get away with it. Stillness, which Richard has, is a great asset on the screen. You don't need to use your voice to the same degree as a stage actor. You don't need to use your body to such a degree. It all has to show in the eye. The slightest movement will speak volumes.

Someday I would love to do a play with Richard on the stage. But I don't think I have the right voice. It's not big enough, though maybe I could train it.

When I was practicing for the poetry reading which Richard and I gave in New York during the *Hamlet* run, Philip Burton, Richard's foster father, made me learn to project my voice even though we were going to be using mikes. He would sit at one side of our hotel room and say to me, "Now pretend I'm at the back end of the theater." I said, "Phil, we're going to have a microphone." He said, "Never mind, you must stand back from the microphone and not depend on it."

I'm not terribly proud of much that I've done as an actress, but I was proud of myself at that poetry reading. It was something I never thought I could do. I didn't think I had the courage to face a live audience for the first time. I knew that eighty-five percent of them had come there and spent a great deal of money to see me fall flat on my face. Richard couldn't really face practicing with me till the night before, because I think he thought I would not be able to make it.

When I rehearsed the poems, I couldn't take my eyes off the page, even though I knew everything by heart. It was almost as if my eyes were on pieces of elastic and were fastened by Scotch tape to the page—and if I removed them, there would be a snap of memory.

The first three minutes on stage I was terrified. I came out in a silk jersey dress and all of a sudden the dress started turning dark from my hands. The sweat was squirting out. But I found, after five minutes, that the adrenalin I'd heard about happened inside me. And all of sudden I became terribly daring, audacious, and I lifted my eyes from the page. There was no snapping of memory. My eyeballs didn't fall out of my head and I looked at the audience and I said whole stanzas and I didn't mess them up. Richard showed his nerves more than I did. He was so nervous for me he kept reading my lines. We both broke up and turned our back on the audience and kind of hid in the curtains. In the week after the poetry reading, we had over a half-million dollars' worth of offers in the U.S. alone—*poetry readings,* mind you.

Actually, I am not satisfied with myself as an entertainer, or whatever one would call a person such as myself. What I would really like is to be good enough for people to think of me as an actress, not a movie star. But it is very difficult once you have become public domain to be taken seriously. Part of me is sorry that I became a public utility.

CHAPTER TEN

THE ELIZABETH TAYLOR who's famous, the one on celluloid, really has no depth or meaning to me. It's a totally superficial working thing, a commodity. I really don't know what the ingredients are exactly—just that it makes money. I'm not even too sure what image the lady from Pismo Beach has of me—except probably she thinks I'm rather scandalous, unstable, a wicked witch with very little feeling—ruthless, fairly lame-brained, determined. Somebody who snaps a finger and gets what she wants.

I really have never tried to analyze why so many people go to my movies. I suppose if people stopped buying the commodity and I cared, I would try to figure out what ingredient was missing.

Most of my films have been melodramatic, so if you like to shed a tear, I suppose you'd like that part of the package. I guess, too, there's that suggestion of the naughty—maybe envy because I've had the honesty to do what some people didn't do at one point in their lives. You might say I'm an escape from diapers and dishwashers—like the boy-meets-girl novelettes.

I genuinely don't think it's because I'm a great beauty. I think Ava Gardner is truly beautiful; I think my daughter Liza is. I think Jacqueline Kennedy is a beautiful woman—tremendous dignity. I am pretty enough. I try not to look like a slob. I don't have a complex about my looks, but I'm too short of leg, too big in the arms, one too many chins, nose a bit crooked, big feet, big hands, I'm too fat. My best feature is my gray hairs. I have them all named; they're all called Burton.

My mother wisely made very sure when I was young that I wouldn't get big-headed about my looks. She said, "You have nice eyes, but they're only nice as long as the expression in back of them is nice. And that depends solely on what you are as a person inside. You are not beautiful, but you can be attractive when you're nice inside."

So I never believed I was pretty. Sometimes she'd pay me a compliment and tell me I was pretty. Afterward she'd kind of laugh about it and say, "It's silly to tell a child that." I agreed with her. Today all I see in the mirror every morning is a face that needs washing.

I do have a flat rule that before publication I clear all photographs of myself, but it has nothing to do with vanity. I have had too much happen to me. They always shoot and print the picture where I'm getting out of the car and my slip shows—or where my mouth is open and you can see my tonsils, as if I were slipping an orange into my throat.

There have, of course, been pictures of myself that I think are okay. But I was either unaware of the camera or the photographer was somebody like Roddy McDowall or Dick Avedon, both of whom I trust completely. I'm just no good trying to relax for photographers I don't know well. That's why there are so many stiff, haughty pictures of me. A frosty curtain comes across my face— a defensive, resentful mask. My lips may move, but it's like the kiss of death. I can't communicate. I become so conscious of the expression on my face, whether my knees are crossed right, whether my petticoat shows. It's awful, as though you're posturing as a caricature of yourself. They say, "Now look sexy." And for the bloody camera I can't. I just can't go "Goo, goo, goo" and part my lips and get that dreamy-eyed look.

Anyway, I am *not* a "sex queen" or a "sex symbol." I really don't think that's why people come to my movies. I don't think I *want* to be one. "Sex symbol" kind of suggests bathrooms in hotels or something. I do know I'm a movie star and I like being a woman. But as far as being thought of as a "sex goddess," I never have been concerned about that. If you're going to be a "sex queen," you do some undressing, some cheesecake, and I've never done any of that.

Maybe Richard and I are sex symbols together because we suggest love. At first, illicit love. And it seems curious that our society today finds illicit love more attractive than married love. Our love is married love now. But there is still a suggestion, I suppose, of rampant sex on the wild.

I can tell you what I think is sexy in a

man. It has to do with warmth, a personal givingness, not self-awareness. Richard is a very sexy man. He's got that sort of jungle essence that one can sense. It's not the way he combs his hair, not the things he wears; and he doesn't think about having muscles.

It's what he says and thinks. When I say that, I don't mean the awful lines some men say—with the tricks with their eyes. You meet some men who probably have been told they have great animal charm. They probably stay awake at night or look into the bathroom mirror thinking, What am I going to say that's going to sound sexy to the next broad? You want to say to them, "Sweetie, pull yourself together."

As far as beauty in a woman is concerned, the thing that can kill it is being too impeccable, too well nurtured, too taken care of, so you can feel the vanity behind it. The kind of beauty where you're afraid to smile too much is a bore. I am sincerely not worried about getting old. Practically all the women I know who were pretty young women became beautiful older women. I think what age and living and experience do to one's face is beautiful. I think a face without flaws, without character, means nothing. I plan on my face having a lot of character in ten years.

But I don't plan on just letting myself go. Whatever happens naturally will happen. I mean if I get fat, I'm not spending years going to masseurs and going on wild diets. Nor am I going, either, to sit down with a box of candies and fudgitate.

Richard and I are really looking forward to the day when we retire, mainly because when that time comes we won't be so famous. Other ex-stars tell me they have funny reactions—all of a sudden you walk into a restaurant and you can't get a table. I don't want to sound ungrateful, because I am very lucky to be successful, but there are many bad things on the other side of the scale—like the constant reminder that you are some kind of a freak. I am still terribly naive. I still believe I have a right to privacy.

I don't think because you are an actor or actress you have any special responsibility to the public just because they want to pry via the press into your private life, make conjectures and decide what kind of a person you are. I owe the public who pays to see me on the screen the best performance I can give. As to how I live my personal life, my responsibility is to the people directly involved with me.

Everything that I have done in my life that is a mistake I will admit is a mistake and answer for it. But I am not going to answer for an image created by hundreds of people who do not know what's true or false. That would take me from here to doomsday.

It really is all too tedious. I mean, who *really* cares? The lady from Pismo Beach, who reads that made-up stuff and believes it, *wants* to believe it and is going to believe it regardless of what she reads. But even if the Pope gave me a testimonial, she would never believe that. I know that I will never be able to be really and truly dignified in the eyes of the public. I shall not be allowed to be.

I did a story with Liza for *Look* magazine. Sweet pictures, and the quotes in the captions came from my heart. I couldn't have believed that people could be as vicious as they were about that in their letters, writing that I couldn't possibly have said those things, that it was inconsistent with my whole character. And if I had had those sentiments, why

205

had I behaved like such an immoral woman all my life? And some of the people said, "Well, quite clearly you can tell from her daughter's expression that she doesn't like her mother." You just can't believe it.

I think it's part of our society to enjoy putting you up on top of the ladder and then taking an animal delight in tearing you to bits. The public seems to revel in the imperfections of the famous, the heroes, and to want to be in a position of attacking—which I guess makes them feel a little bit superior. So I should have delighted lots of fans throughout the world. If anybody has given them an opportunity to feel superior, I have.

I do have an enormous guilt complex about being divorced three times. For example, I have a terrible thing about nuns and priests, though I never met one who wasn't nice to me. On the ship coming over from Europe, three nuns passed our table every day, smiled at everybody else, but seemed to ignore Richard and me. Of course, always the masochist, I decided they were cutting us dead. One morning while I was combing my hair, I had a Walter Mitty about it. In my daydream the major-domo let them know I had asked questions about them. The nuns came over and asked if they could answer any questions. I told them that their faces were always so smiling, but when they came past us, they looked as though they smelled something bad. And then I caught myself in this perfectly dreadful "daymare," something I *never* would have done in real life. And I was appalled at what a swamp of guilt this showed.

That day at lunch I desperately wanted them to smile. And, you know, they did—and the first two said good morning. At that moment, it was like a sort of benediction.

I have often wondered what kind of a person I would be today if I did not have these enormous guilts—if everything had gone easily and I had not made such horrific mistakes. I think I would have been the most awful, pontifical Goody Two Shoes. I was really so smug, so sweet, so good, so spoiled—so intolerant of anybody else's downfall.

But tragedy, mistakes, shame for your mistakes cannot leave you untouched. All the superficial things that one gave such value to before—money, luxury, indulging in whims—calamity makes them seem so incidental. I swear to God I'd be just as happy living with Richard and my kids in a shack. And I treat the happiness I have now with great respect, great appreciation, because I know how fragile and precarious it is—how easily it can go. I am more aware that happiness is a composite total, that it is not some sort of sweet, safe heaven. To mean anything, it *must* include unhappiness. For me to see this is like being given a whole new world.